C0-CCF-024

BRITISH MASTERS OF MEDICINE

BRITISH MASTERS OF MEDICINE

EDITED BY
SIR D'ARCY POWER

Essay Index Reprint Series

BOOKS FOR LIBRARIES PRESS
FREEPORT, NEW YORK

First Published 1936

Reprinted 1969

STANDARD BOOK NUMBER:
8369-1375-2

LIBRARY OF CONGRESS CATALOG CARD NUMBER:
79-99721

PRINTED IN THE UNITED STATES OF AMERICA

PREFACE

THE injunction to praise famous men and to speak of our predecessors seems to have been implanted in the human breast from the very earliest times. In the Stone Age when the man was not engaged in hunting he spent the whole of his leisure in celebrating his ancestors. This we learn from the Australian aborigines who spend weeks and months in the performance of ceremonies by which they hand down the memory of those from whom they were descended. It is not until after initiation that the younger men are allowed to share the knowledge which in turn they are to hand on to the next generation.

In Egypt the Pyramids kept great names alive, whilst in Greece the "Iliad" and "Odyssey" and in Rome the "Aeneid" record many whose names and deeds would long since have been forgotten. The great Sagas in like manner tell us of heroes and their deeds. The houes and barrows, the white horses and many place-names have done similar service in our own country. All who are thus handed down to us were famous in their generation and were considered worthy of remembrance. They indeed are legendary but later came the chroniclers, men like Froissart who wrote of heroes and made them live for those who can read and appreciate their mighty deeds. They were all of the military caste like their mythical predecessors. Later still the circle widened and the number of those worthy to be remembered became so great that they had to be classified and arranged in biographical dictionaries.

Such accounts have left their light burning in England, in the United States, in France and in Germany.

The articles in this book are written by those who have been attached to the great institutions which their heroes made famous. They appeared originally in the pages of the *Medical Press & Circular*, as a series of articles under the title of " British Masters of Medicine," and were published during the years 1934 and 1935. They are of such excellence that it seemed a pity to allow them to sink into the oblivion which is the inevitable fate of all contributions to periodical literature. It was felt, too, that many who did not read the articles when they first appeared would be glad to have the opportunity of now doing so.

The title makes it clear that the volume is limited to great men who have worked in England, Scotland and Ireland. The chapters are arranged in chronological order with some additions and minor corrections of the original articles. The record proves that the flame of genius still burns fiercely amongst us and the praise of these men is an incentive to their successors. To some extent also the contributions of the various authors give an account of the progress of medicine and science from Harvey to Starling.

D'ARCY POWER.

LONDON,
May, 1936.

CONTENTS

LIST OF ILLUSTRATIONS

AUTHORS

D. McC. A. . D. McCrae Aitken, F.R.C.S., Director of Surgery at the Robert Jones & Agnes Hunt Orthopædic Hospital.

J. J. A. . . . J. Johnston Abraham, C.B.E., D.S.O., F.R.C.S., Senior Surgeon to the Princess Beatrice Hospital.

B. B. . . . Sir Buckston Browne, F.R.C.S., Hunterian Trustee and Gold Medallist, Royal College of Surgeons of England.

C. B. . . . Sir Charlton Briscoe, Bart., M.D., F.R.C.P., Senior Physician to King's College Hospital.

†W. B.-B. . William Blair-Bell [*d.* 1936], Emeritus Professor of Obstetrics and Gynæcology, University of Liverpool.

J. D. C. . . John D. Comrie, M.D., F.R.C.P.Ed., F.S.A., Physician to the Royal Infirmary and Lecturer on the History of Medicine in the University of Edinburgh.

T. E. . . . Terence C. F. East, M.D., F.R.C.P., Physician to King's College Hospital.

C. L. E. . . Charles A. Lovatt Evans, F.R.C.P., D.Sc., Jodrell Professor of Physiology, University College, London.

G. E. G. . . Geo. E. Gask, F.R.C.S., Emeritus Professor of Surgery, University of London, Consulting Surgeon to St. Bartholomew's Hospital.

J. A. G. . . James Andrew Gunn, M.A., M.D., D.Sc., Professor of Pharmacology, University of Oxford.

A. F. H. . . Arthur F. Hurst, D.M., F.R.C.P., Senior Physician to Guy's Hospital.

A. K. . . . Sir Arthur Keith, F.R.S., Master of the Buckston Browne Research Farm, formerly Conservator of the Hunterian Museum, Royal College of Surgeons of England.

H. W. L. . . H. Willoughby Lyle, M.D., F.R.C.S., Consulting Ophthalmic Surgeon to King's College and the Royal Eye Hospitals.

H. MacC.. . Henry MacCormac, C.B.E., M.D., F.R.C.P., Physician to the Dermatological Department, the Middlesex Hospital.

P. H. M.-B. . Philip H. Manson-Bahr, D.S.O., F.R.C.P., Physician to the Hospital for Tropical Diseases.

T. G. M. . . Thomas Gillman Moorhead, M.D., F.R.C.P.I., Regius Professor of Physic, Trinity College, Dublin; Past President of the Royal College of Physicians, Ireland.

D'A. P. . . Sir D'Arcy Power, K.B.E., F.R.C.S., F.S.A., Consulting Surgeon and Archivist to St. Bartholomew's Hospital; Hunterian Trustee, Royal College of Surgeons of England.

E. G. R. . . Miss Edith Gittings Reid, Author of "The Life of Sir William Osler."

R. H. O. B. R. Ronald Henry Ottwell Betham Robinson, F.R.C.S.Eng., Surgeon to Out-Patients, St. Thomas's Hospital.

H. D. R. . . Sir Humphry Davy Rolleston, Bart., G.C.V.O., K.C.B., M.D., Past President of the Royal College of Physicians, London; Emeritus Regius Professor of Physic, Cambridge.

H. R. T. . . Henry Reynolds Thompson, M.A., M.B., F.R.C.S., the London Hospital.

†T. T. . . . THEODORE THOMPSON, M.A., M.D., F.R.C.P., F.R.C.S. [*d.* 1935], Physician to London Hospital.

S. T. . . . SIR STCLAIR THOMSON, M.D., F.R.C.P., Emeritus Professor of Laryngology and Consulting Physician to King's College Hospital.

C. P. G. W. . CECIL P. G. WAKELEY, F.R.C.S., Surgeon to King's College Hospital.

D. W. . . DAVID WATERSTON, M.D., F.R.C.S.Edin., Bute Professor of Anatomy, St. Andrew's University, N.B.

WILLIAM HARVEY
1578–1657
(From the portrait in the Royal College of Physicians of London)

To face p. 1

I WILLIAM HARVEY
(1578–1657)

EXPERIMENTAL PHYSIOLOGY

ONE hundred years before the birth of John Hunter, Harvey's discovery of the circulation was published, in 1628, when he was fifty years of age. It was fitting that great scientists should arise at a period recognised as precocious in literature, art and philosophy, adorned by such names as Shakespeare, Milton, Rubens, Van Dyck, Bacon.

During Harvey's lifetime there were events of political importance and excitement such as seldom befall an individual. The first twenty-five years were passed while Queen Elizabeth was on the throne. In the next two reigns, of James I and Charles I, Harvey was physician-in-ordinary to both monarchs; but after the surrender of the latter the remainder of Harvey's life was spent in retirement during that time of repression by the Commonwealth. Revolutions occurred both in religion and society, the spread of Calvinism and the ruin of the Royalist country landowners by fines, lost estates and so forth. It is a matter of wonder that mental detachment could have been carried so far under these circumstances as to allow of concentration sufficient to make the discoveries that he did. For the greatness of Harvey's work lies not so much in the actual discovery of the circulation as in the revolution of thought and method for which he was responsible.

William Harvey was born at Folkestone, April 1st, 1578. In spite of attempts to place the date as April 2nd, there is little doubt that the unpropitious April 1st was correct. At the age of ten, when in accordance with the education of the period he could probably speak Latin and read Greek, he went to the King's School, Canterbury. This was the year 1588, in which the Spanish Armada was defeated, and no doubt the boy would have been caught up in the excitement and flurry at Folkestone, where the town was liable for a levy. We hear nothing of him at Canterbury. At sixteen years of age he went to Caius College, Cambridge, the medical college, with a scholarship of £3 0*s*. 8*d*. per annum. He took his degree in 1597, four years later. In those days Harvey's education was probably up to this point not in scientific subjects, but in classics, divinity and logic, although Dr. Caius' reputation for having introduced the study of anatomy to this country drew prospective students of medicine to that college. It was after taking his degree at Cambridge that Harvey proceeded to Padua, where Fabricius had succeeded Fallopius, who followed Vessalius as lecturer on anatomy and surgery. At Padua, Harvey worked for four years till 1602, when he left with the degree of Doctor of Medicine. He represented the Englishmen at Padua, 1600–2, on the Students' Council. No doubt, on this account, as being one of the more important students, he was entitled to a stemma or tablet, which was actually discovered at Padua in 1893.

On returning to England, he took his Doctor of Medicine degree at Cambridge, and two years later (1604) was admitted a candidate to the College, and in 1607 was elected a Fellow of the Royal College of Physicians. He was now practising in London, and in 1608 he applied for the reversion of the post of physician to St. Bartholomew's Hospital held by Dr. Wilkinson. Harvey is mentioned frequently in the records of St. Bartholomew's Hospital, and on this occasion it is noted that his application, backed by the President and other Fellows of the College of Physicians, as well as by His Majesty the King, was granted. This appointment corresponded to the post of assistant physician. Dr. Wilkinson died the year following, and the record runs :

"*13th October*, 1609.

"In Presence of Sir John Spencer, Knight, President, and others

"Dr. Harvey.

"This day, Mr. William Harvey, Doctor of Physic, is admitted to the office of Physician of this Hospital, which Mr. Dr. Wilkinson, deceased, late held, according to a former grant to him made and the charge of the said office has been read unto him."

He received £25 per annum, and later an additional sum of £8 6*s*. 8*d*. because he was not residing in a house which went with the office.

We hear little of Harvey for the next six years, till, in 1615, he was appointed Lumleian lecturer, a life appointment, to deliver two lectures per week all the year round. This was a lectureship founded in 1581 by Lord Lumley and Dr. Caldwell, and though the terms of the appointment are altered, Lumleian lectures are still delivered at the Royal College of Physicians. Some of the notes of his lectures are preserved in the British Museum. He mixed up English and Latin phrases in an illegible jumble, but the notes show that as early as 1616, Harvey had grasped the principle of the circulation. It was not till 1628 that he published the full story, "Exercitatio Anatomica de Motu Cordis et Sanguinis in animalibus," but when he did so he was regarded as a crank and lost much of the practice he had built up. Evidently during this period, 1609–28, Harvey had made a reputation, and in 1618 he was appointed physician extraordinary to King James I. He was attending the King prior to his death, for in 1626 he was examined by the House of Commons on a suggestion that he had poisoned James I, who had died in 1625. He was completely exonerated.

Harvey was also an intimate friend of Charles I, whom he kept acquainted with many of his investigations. In one case where a patient with a large sinus in the chest was referred to Harvey, he demonstrated this individual to the King, and both of them felt the heart contracting and dilating, and made the observation that there was no sensation conveyed to the patient by their manipulations. He attended King Charles when he went to Scotland for his coronation in 1625, and subsequently on other occasions. He there received the Freedom both of Edinburgh and Aberdeen. During the Civil War he was sometimes with the King and sometimes in London, and on more than one occasion received a pass through the Parliamentary forces either to the King or some patient who wanted to see him in London. Later such passage was denied him by Cromwell. He was with the King's forces at Edgehill (1642), and during the battle was sitting under a hedge with two of the young princes reading a book, but being within cannon fire he had to interrupt his reading and move. He was at Oxford while the city was holding out for the King, and during this time was investigating the development of the chick in the egg with George Bathurst, a Fellow of Trinity College, " who had a hen to hatch eggs in his chamber which they opened daily to see the progress and way of generation." It is not known whether he was with the King at his execution. It is unlikely, for he seems to have taken little interest in public affairs after 1646, and retired. He died in 1657 in his eightieth year.

Such is a brief epitome of the life of Harvey. He was

stated to be of medium stature, white haired at sixty; he was short-tempered, and evidently did not suffer fools gladly, although he conducted controversy with consideration for his opponents. He was not a great success as a practitioner, had no reputation as a therapeutist, and after the publication of his book, in 1628, lost a large part of his practice. He was not subjected to financial worries, his father was apparently well off, and his brothers successful business men, who looked after Harvey's affairs in a satisfactory manner.

He married the daughter of Dr. Lancelot Browne, physician to Queen Elizabeth, in 1604. Nothing more is known of her, and there were no children. She predeceased him. He was a strong supporter of the College of Physicians, being elected censor in 1613, 1625 and 1629. In 1620 he was treasurer. In 1627 he was made one of the eight elect who examined candidates for qualification, and from whom one was chosen as President. In 1654, Harvey, in his absence, was chosen as President. He attended the comitia of the College on the following day, and after thanking his colleagues for this honour proceeded to decline it on account of his age and infirmity. In 1656, the year before his death, he made over to the College as a free gift his country estate at Burmarsh, in Kent, yielding £56 a year. The object of this was to institute an annual feast at which the beneficiaries of the College should be commemorated in a Latin oration, to provide some payment for the orator, and to make provision for the keeper of the library and museum. Previously he had provided a building containing a large room in which the Fellows could meet, and above this a library. The latter he had furnished with books on science, natural history and travel, surgical instruments and numerous objects of curiosity, and in 1653, at a feast, Harvey entertained the President and Fellows and handed the title-deeds over to the College.

Such was his fondness for the College that he left a clause in his Will directing that sufficient money was to be raised to pay for the completion of the building which he had begun to erect within the College of Physicians.

For some years prior to his death Harvey had suffered severely from gout. He had, however, continued in the office of Lumleian lecturer until the summer of 1656, and discharged the duties conscientiously. He had lived to see his work on the circulation universally accepted. He had for some years been making investigations into the generation of insects. The notes of these observations, his museum, etc., were ransacked by soldiers in 1642, whereby notes of great value were said to have been destroyed. He continued working on generation till his researches, in 1651, were published at the request of Dr. Ent. He did not obtain results comparable to those with the circulation. It is seldom given to one man to make more than a single notable advance in science. However, some four or five years before his death he had realised that it was not wise for a man of his age to be engaged in investigations of new and difficult questions. Otherwise he remained in the possession of his full faculties until the day of his death, June 3rd, 1657, when he evidently had a cerebral hæmorrhage, the gradual onset of which led him to realise what was happening, so that he sent for his nephews, to each of whom he gave some token by which he should be remembered.

His funeral was delayed until June 25th, when the procession started from London followed by a large number of Fellows of the College of Physicians. He was buried at Hempstead, in Essex, about fifty miles from London, in an outer chapel built by his brother on the north side of the church. His body was wrapped in a leaden case and was placed between the bodies of two nieces. In 1847 the window in this vault had gone to pieces, and it was seen that the lead shell had also suffered from exposure to wind and rain. In 1868 the vault was repaired. In 1878 the question of removing the remains of Harvey to Westminster Abbey was considered. In the winter of 1882 the tower of the church fell without injuring the Harvey chapel. However, an examination of the shell showed the lead to be perishing rapidly, and after consideration by a committee of the College of Physicians Harvey's remains were carried from the vault and deposited in a sarcophagus in the chapel above the vault. Recently further repairs to the tower of the church have been carried out, largely assisted by grants from the Fellows of the College of Physicians.

To appreciate the greatness of Harvey's achievement in discovering the circulation of the blood, we have to consider the conditions of the times. There was the political situation, full of uncertainty, and the religious revival leading to Calvinism ; the education of the age was largely classical, living on the importance of precedent and the sayings of the ancients, and culminating in the bondage to Galen, whose writings were accepted almost as heaven-sent and not to be disputed, or even doubted. There was the difficulty in getting subjects for dissection, a difficulty which certainly was diminishing, and the absence of implements for investigation, glass tubing, time recorders and so forth. This was before the time of microscopes and watches with second hands, and though magnifying glasses were in use, time was often reckoned as the interval between beginning and ending of a psalm or prayer. There were, too, the accepted views of the functions of the organs of the body to overcome. It was held that there were two kinds of blood : arterial, conveying heat and vital spirits, and venous, manufactured in the liver from food absorbed from the intestines, nourishing the body; that valves slowed the onward flow of blood; that blood ebbed and flowed in the heart and arteries, being pressed out in systole and drawn back in diastole, acquiring properties while in the heart which were dissipated to the body. It was realised that blood had to get from the right ventricle to the left. It was admitted that some went through the lungs, mainly to nourish them, while the greater portion passed through pores in the interventricular septum. The presence of these pores was postulated and accepted, although not seen in the dead body, but "reason assures us, however, that such pores exist." The function of the lungs was to cool the blood lest it became too heated in the heart. The anatomist who made an observation had to correlate this with the writings of Galen or Aristotle, and it amounted to heresy to make a statement which such authority did not justify. It is true that Cæsalpinus, 1593, had appreciated the pulmonary circulation. His statements were not based on logical deductions and made no impression on the teaching of the time.

Harvey's work may be summed up in words from his own preface: ". . . because I profess both to learn and to teach anatomy not from books but from dissections, not from the positions of philosophers, but from the fabric of nature." He stressed the identity of structure and function of the right and left sides of the heart and of the blood each contained. He observed the sequence of contraction of auricle and ventricle, and deduced the filling of the ventricle by the auricle, the drive of blood to the aorta by the ventricle, and the function of the valves in preventing regurgitation, and recognised that systole was a muscular contraction, and was the important act, not diastole, as hitherto contended.

He knew from comparative anatomy of the single ventricle, related it to the condition in pre-natal mammalian life, and deduced the pulmonary circulations from the changes occurring after birth. He compared the passage of blood through the lungs to percolation of urine through the kidney or sweat through glands. From this he deduced the analogy of the systemic circulation. (It was accepted that blood from the portal vein passed through the liver to the right auricle for the reason that this was the only course open to it, and this made acceptance of these heretical theories possible.) He confirms this " circulation " by mathematical calculation, showing that more blood passes through the heart than could be obtained from food, that blood is impelled to the arteries as a continuous stream, and that blood is being returned by the veins in a like manner. Then follows the estimation of the quantity of blood passing through the heart as being greater than that obtained by exsanguinating. He then turns to experiment, the collapse of veins when there is extensive arterial bleeding, and the failure of bleeding from an artery if the aorta is obstructed, the distension of veins and emptiness of the heart and aorta when the cava is obstructed ; and the distension of veins and heart and emptiness of arteries when the obstruction is applied to the aorta. This confirmed the pump action of the heart, the intake from the veins, the supply to the aorta. He then uses the knowledge obtained from applying a tourniquet to a limb, so obstructing the veins. When the tourniquet is tight enough to obstruct the pulse there is no swelling of hand or veins, but when less tight so that the pulse is felt, the hand swells and the veins are distended, clearly showing that blood comes by the arteries, the veins being obstructed in both instances. From the fact that in phlebotomy the patient faints from draining of the vascular system in the course of half an hour, it follows that all the blood in the body must have passed through the limb in this time. He then demonstrates the function of valves in the veins to prevent blood passing from the big to little veins, and finally sums up the results of his investigations that the sole function of the heart is to keep sending the blood round the body. This is a complete explanation and logical conclusion of the results of the observations.

To us, three hundred years later, when some knowledge of physiology is taught in every school, the wonder is that there ever had been this lack of knowledge of the circulation. We have been brought up on the milk of investigation and trial and error. The glory of Harvey's work is that he discovered and introduced this new method without which the rapid advance in science would not have been possible. It was a one-man revolution in procedure.

This greatest of physiologists is commemorated each year by the Royal College of Physicians, of which he is the ornament, by observing the terms of his bequest. When conveying the estate at Burmash to the College he directed among other things that once every year an oration shall be made to commemorate benefactors and to " exhort the Fellows to search and study out the secrets of nature by way of experiment." Also he directed that on the same day " a general feast shall be kept within the College for all Fellows that shall please to come." On St. Luke's day the Harveian Oration is delivered and is followed by the dinner, thus fulfilling the instructions. Harvey realised the advantage to the College and to the honour and dignity of the profession of mutual love and affection—never more true than to-day—and reminded the Fellows that " concordia res parvae crescunt, discordia magnae dilabuntur."

C. B.

THOMAS SYDENHAM
1624–1689

To face p. 11

II THOMAS SYDENHAM

(1624–1689)

CLINICAL MEDICINE

AMONG the prominent physicians in Britain during the seventeenth century, such as William Harvey (1578–1657), Francis Glisson (1597–1677), Thomas Willis (1621–75), and Richard Lower (1631–91), the outstanding figure in clinical practice was Thomas Sydenham (1624–89)—the "British Hippocrates." He was one of the great triumvirate of British medicine represented in the libraries of two former regius professors of medicine at Oxford, Sir Henry Acland (1815–1900) and Sir William Osler (1849–1919), by their portraits on a panel with the legends: "Linacre: Litteræ. Harvey: Scientia. Sydenham: Praxis."

Breaking with authority, he drew living pictures of disease from observation of patients, and not from the tomes of the medical fathers, for, as he said, it was his "nature to think where others read." His attention was almost confined to the works of Hippocrates—whom he called "the divine old man"—Cicero, Francis Bacon, and to "Don Quixote," which we can picture him recommending with an inscrutable if not somewhat ironical smile to the pedantic poetaster, Sir Richard Blackmore (1653–1729), in response to the appeal, What ought to be read? The meaning of this rather disconcerting advice was probably merely that medicine was not to be learned from books, and that one book was therefore as good as another. He took men back to the clinical medicine of Hippocrates, just as his senior, William Harvey, had led them back to Galen's physiology. From bedside study of their natural history he distinguished scarlet fever from measles, rheumatism from gout, and gave the classical descriptions of chorea (" Sydenham's chorea ") and hysteria, emphasising the essentials and keeping the immaterial details in due proportion.

Hypotheses and philosophical systems he detested, and he had a low opinion of the prevalent iatro-chemical doctrines. Regarding diseases as species, like those of animals and plants, he was the founder of scientific nosology, and the protagonist in the seventeenth century of the specificity of acute diseases, for which he was later much criticised ; he urged a search for specific remedies, though the only one he recognised and prescribed was cinchona, or Jesuit's bark, for ague. Sydenham was born a few years before the therapeutic use of cinchona became known to Europeans, and these two events have recently been appropriately commemorated ; the tercentenary of Sydenham's birth was celebrated, in 1924, at the Royal College of Physicians of London and at the Académie de Médecine of Paris, where Professor A. Chauffard (1855–1932) suggested that Trousseau (1801–67) might be called " the French Sydenham." Six years later, in December, 1930, the International tercentenary celebration of the discovery of cinchona was held at the Wellcome Historical Medical Museum in London. Sydenham also advocated a definite system of treatment on rational grounds, instead of polypharmacy ; firmly believed in the inherent curative power of nature ; practised the cooling treatment of smallpox, which appears to have been a *via media* between the method promoting the eruption by blankets and brandy, and that of venesection and purgation ; and greatly valued laudanum as a remedy. His pupil, Thomas Dover (1660–1742), buccaneer, retriever of Alexander Selkirk ("Robinson Crusoe") in 1710, and "quick-silver" doctor, remembered his master's injunctions when in 1732 he published the formula of Pulvis ipecacuanhæ compositus, with its opium content.

In spite of his strong condemnation of speculative explanations, Sydenham had, from close observation of the epidemics of acute disease occurring in London, formed very definite views about the variations in their character, and followed in the steps of Hippocrates and Guillaume de Baillou (1538–1616), of Paris, who wrote about "the epidemic constitutions" of the years 1570 to 1579. He elaborated this doctrine to the effect that an external influence—telluric or climatic—becomes dominant, and is responsible for some peculiar clinical manifestations to the exclusion of other symptoms, and that these different types of epidemics, for example, in 1661–4, malarial, in 1663–6, like plague, and in 1666–9, suggesting smallpox, recur at intervals of years. The rather mysterious term "epidemic constitutions" has been used in different senses, but the clearest translation is that given by Major Greenwood, namely, that the non-specific secondary infections, such as those so familiar in influenza and measles, are as important as regards morbidity and mortality as the specific agents of the disease. Shortly after the War there was a renewal of interest in the subject of the epidemic constitutions, and Sydenham was hailed as the "founder of the modern science of epidemiology." Though never attached to any of the few London hospitals then in existence, he had two pupils whose names at least are household words: Dover, mentioned already, and Sir Hans Sloane (1660–1753), who, though President of both the Royal Society and the Royal College of Physicians of London, and founder of the

British Museum, is nominally more familiar to the man in Hans Place and the adjacent street for other and fairly obvious reasons.

The Man and His Character

Sydenham was a very independent character, and this may have been accentuated by the fact that whereas he was a Puritan, most of his contemporaries at Oxford in the Royal Society, and at the Royal College of Physicians of London, were adherents of the Stuarts. His position may perhaps be illustrated by comparing him with Thomas Willis (1621–75), who was at Oxford with him, and was afterwards a very successful practitioner in London, and author of many important clinical treatises. On his return in 1647 to loyalist Oxford, Sydenham, who had been a trooper and captain in Cromwell's army, was not a member of the "Philosophicall Clubbe," which met in Wadham, and was closely associated with the "invisible college" in London, out of which the Royal Society developed in 1662. He was never a fellow of the Royal Society or of the Royal College of Physicians of London, though he was a licentiate (the membership was not established until 1859) from June 25th, 1663. The real explanation of what would otherwise appear to be a grave omission on the part of the College is that until 1676, when, on April 14th, he proceeded to the degree of M.D. at Pembroke College, Cambridge, probably because his eldest son, William, was in residence there, the statutes of the Royal College of Physicians made it impossible to elect him a fellow. Even then he would, at the age of fifty-two years, have had to undergo an examination and to make an application for this privilege. This he never did, and his failing health may have had some influence in this respect, for during the first three months of 1677 he was unable to practise owing to a severe attack of gout and hæmaturia, and then was in the country convalescing until the autumn. Willis, on the other hand, was prominent in all these societies; he was a member of the "Philosophicall Clubbe" at Oxford, which Norman Moore aptly called "the circle of Willis," was elected a Fellow of the Royal Society on November 18th, 1663, and an honorary fellow of the Royal College of Physicians of London in December, 1664. Sydenham, however, had many firm friends among the Royalists, such as Robert Boyle, described as "the seventh son of the earl of Cork and the Father of Modern Chemistry," and John Locke, and also at the Royal College of Physicians.

The Sydenhams were an old West Country family, of Sydenham, near Bridgwater, Somerset, going back to the time of King John; the Dorsetshire branch owned an estate at Wynford Eagle, near Rampisham, the birthplace of Francis Glisson (1597–1677); here Thomas was born in September, 1624, as the fourth son of William Sydenham. On May 20th, 1642, he matriculated at Magdalen Hall (now Hertford College), then the centre of Puritanism in Royalist Oxford; but he did not stay long, for civil war broke out in August, and after the battle of Edgehill on October 23rd, 1642, when Oxford was garrisoned for Charles I, he joined the Parliamentary Forces with three of his brothers; he was wounded, and imprisoned in Exeter. In 1646 he was on his way back to Oxford without any thought of entering on the "physic line," and when passing through London and visiting his brother William, a colonel and later a Privy Councillor, who was ill, he met Thomas Coxe (1615–85), physician to the Parliamentary Army, and President of the Royal College of Physicians for one year (1682), being then, it is said, deprived of that office because he was "whiggishly inclined." This was a momentous meeting, for, influenced by Coxe, Sydenham decided to take up medicine. He returned to Magdalen Hall, but soon migrated to Wadham. He was created a bachelor of medicine on April 14th, 1648, though he did not take a degree in Arts, and on the following October 3rd, was elected a fellow of All Souls, where he was senior bursar (1649), and the friend of Thomas Millington (1624–1704), afterwards (1696–1704) President of the College of Physicians. In 1655 he married, resigned his fellowship, and some time before 1661 removed to London. In the interval, perhaps about 1659, he visited Montpellier, where he foregathered with Charles Barbeyrac (1629–99), the popular teacher, a Protestant, and also an ardent disciple of Hippocrates.

A sufferer from gout, that *opprobrium medicorum*, from the age of thirty, he gave, in 1683, an unsurpassed description of the acute phases, in which he said: "for humble individuals like myself there is one poor comfort, which is this, viz., that gout, unlike any other disease, kills more rich men than poor, more wise men than simple." When thirty-seven years of age he began to suffer from urinary calculus, and Erasmus' epigram: "I have renal colic, you have gout; we have married sisters," makes Sydenham doubly unfortunate. These gained on him, and after suffering a number of these attacks and hæmaturia he died at his house in Pall Mall on December 29th, 1689, and was buried in St. James's Church, Piccadilly, where in 1810 a tablet, describing him as "Medicus in omme aevum nobilis," was erected to his memory by the Royal College of Physicians of London.

H. D. R.

1649–1734

A line drawing, found in a volume in the Bodleian Library—said to be the only known portrait of Floyer.

To face p. 17

III SIR JOHN FLOYER
(1649–1734)

HYDROTHERAPIST

"Eques medicus, apud exteros vir non satis notus . . . meretur magis innotescere."—HALLER.

JOHN FLOYER was born at Hints Hall, near Lichfield in Staffordshire, on April 25th, 1649, and died in Lichfield in 1734. He therefore spanned exactly the interval between William Harvey and John Hunter, overlapping the lives of each by six years.

Floyer matriculated at Queen's College, Oxford, June 10th, 1664, aged fifteen, and graduated B.A. in 1668, M.A. in 1671, B.M. in 1674, and D.M. in 1680. He tells us that he spent twelve years in Oxford, after which time he settled in Lichfield as a physician. Little is known of his life in Oxford apart from the scanty references in his own books, and one can only speculate as to influences under which he came while he lived in Queen's College. Oxford at that time offered but scanty facilities for medical study. There was a Regius Professor of Medicine, whose duties were to read a lecture twice weekly from the text of Hippocrates or Galen. About half a century before Floyer began the study of medicine in Oxford a Readership in Anatomy had been established. It was aptly called a Readership because it was not till a century after Floyer's student days that medical students had to produce evidence that they had attended one entire dissection and one lecture on the skeleton. Boyle brought Stahl to Oxford to teach chemistry in 1659. Floyer's medical teaching must therefore have consisted chiefly of lectures on anatomy and chemistry and of readings from the texts of Hippocrates and Galen. Added to this he was, like many physicians of his time, a good classical scholar. With this apparently inadequate medical training, suffering all his life from asthma and living the life of a busy practitioner in Lichfield, he made many original contributions to medical science such as entitle him to a permanent and high place in the history of medicine. Haller's reproach, quoted above, still stands, because Floyer's work has never been sufficiently recognised even in his own country.

Though routine medical teaching in Oxford was then, from a modern point of view, hopelessly inadequate, the period of Floyer's residence (1664–76) marked the close of a time of great intellectual activity in the University. It is doubtful whether any university in any country at any time can point to a group of alumni so eminent for the brilliance and permanence of their scientific achievements as can Oxford at the time of the Restoration. The day was drawing to a close when men could take all knowledge for their province ; but the sun set in splendour.

When, a boy of fifteen, Floyer matriculated at Queen's College in 1664, whom would he meet ? Sydenham and Wren had left Oxford in 1661. Boyle may not have left Oxford till 1668. Lower went from Oxford to London in 1666 and published his " Tractatus de Corde " in 1669. Willis published his " Cerebri Anatome " in 1664, and went to London two years later. Locke, who entered Christ Church in 1651, and after the Restoration " entered on the physic line and got some business at Oxford," took the degree of B.M. in 1674. Halley entered Queen's College the year before Floyer left it. Mayow, a Fellow of All Souls, was in Oxford almost the whole period of Floyer's residence there, and published his "Tractatus de Respiratione" in 1668. Sydenham, Wren, Boyle, Lower, Willis, Locke, Halley, Mayow—all almost within a decade. Little wonder, perhaps, that Floyer's active mind was directed to scientific enquiry; there was something here to infuse life into the dry bones of Hippocrates and Galen.

Of Floyer's life in Lichfield but little is known, though some knowledge of the position he held may be gathered from various sources. Ten years after he returned to Lichfield (1686) he was made a Justice of the Peace for his natural life. Later he became a Bailiff, and by 1728 Senior Bailiff of the city. He was knighted by the King at Whitehall on January 24th, 1684–5, and it is noted that he was then living at Lichfield. This was before any of his books were published and before he had gained eminence in his profession. It seems probable, therefore, that he was knighted for political services. In 1687 James II, in the course of a tour through England, arrived at Lichfield, and was met by Sir John Floyer among others. The morning after his arrival (September 1st, 1687) in the cathedral church the King touched several persons for "the Evil." This incident may have influenced Floyer in favour of touching for the Evil; in any case, among the 200 persons touched by Queen Anne, on March 30th, 1714, for scrofula, one was Samuel Johnson, whose mother in this application was influenced by the advice of Sir John Floyer, "then an eminent physician and who practised in Lichfield." Perhaps some reference to Floyer's connection with Johnson may be of general interest. Some of Floyer's books were published by Samuel's father, Michael Johnson, bookseller, of Lichfield. Medical terms in Johnson's dictionary were taken partly from the works of Floyer. Johnson, a few months before his death, borrowed from the cathedral library at Lichfield, on July 17th, 1704, Floyer's "Treatise on Asthma," in the hope of finding a remedy for the same disease. He kept it till November 9th. There is still a copy of Floyer's book on asthma in the Cathedral library at Lichfield, but it contains no marginal comments by Johnson. From other evidence it is probable that Floyer was one of Johnson's physicians. Johnson evidently thought highly of him, and strongly pressed the editor of Nichol's "Literary Anecdotes" to give to the public some account of the life and works of Floyer, "whose learning and piety, the doctor said, deserve recording."

Though, as late as 1812, it was stated that "an original portrait of Floyer is preserved at Lichfield," this portrait is not now recognised. While looking through a copy of Harwood's "History and Antiquities of the Church and City of Lichfield" in the Bodleian Library, I was fortunate in discovering a line drawing of Floyer loosely interpolated in the volume. This is the drawing here reproduced, and is the only portrait of Floyer known. It may be a drawing from the portrait in Lichfield, in which case it may lead to identification of the original. In appearance Floyer was tall and of spare habit.

It will be possible here to refer only to Floyer's chief contributions to medicine and physiology. The writer hopes to publish a fuller account of his life and works from materials collected for the last twenty years.

In 1707 Floyer published his first book on "The Physician's Pulse-Watch, or an Essay to Explain the Old Art of Feeling the Pulse, and to improve it by the help of a Pulse-Watch." The aim and scope of this book are sufficiently outlined in his Preface to it. "I have for many years try'd Pulses by the minute in Common Watches, and Pendulum Clocks, when I was among my patients; after some time I met with the common Sea-Minute-Glass, which I used for my Cold Bathing, and by that I made most of my experiments ; but because that was not portable I caused a Pulse-Watch to be made which run 60 seconds, and I placed it in a box to be more easily carried, and by this I now feel pulses." The instrument itself was " made and sold by Mr. Samuel Watson, Watchmaker, in Long Acre, by Sir John Floyer's Direction," but no specimen of it seems to have survived.

The nature of Floyer's observations on the pulse is summarised by him as follows : " All I pretend to is the discovery of a Rule whereby we may know the natural Pulse, and the Excesses and Defects from that in Diseases ; and from the Pulse we may take our Indications for the use of Diet and Medicine ; as I shall prove hereafter. . . . The most useful distinction of Pulses, and the most certain, is the difference we observe of the numbers of the Pulse, in a minute ; the most natural Pulse will have from 70 to 75 in a minute in perfect health. . . . The lowest pulse I have counted is 55, the highest 132 . . . but 'tis certain fewer may be counted and more."

Floyer not only initiated the practice of counting the pulse by the minute, but made a large number of observations on the pulse rate as affected by age, sex, emotions, diet, climate, temperature, drugs and disease. His observations are of unequal merit and lose much for want of proper arrangement, for which he apologises : " I having no health to transcribe what I have writ." Two contributions which he made to the physiology of the circulation have been lost sight of, and may be briefly mentioned here. So far as I know, Floyer was the first to attempt to estimate the blood volume and to compare it with the body-weight. " I have found by divers experiments that one Pound and a-half of blood at least may be allowed to every twenty Pound of the whole Body, and the quantity of Blood in a man of a Hundred and Sixty Pound Weight is at least thirteen Pound." This ratio between blood and body weight (1 to 12 or 13) found by Floyer is remarkably near that which has been found by more modern and more elaborate experiments. From another experiment, in which he injected water, " by Sir Sam. Morelands Hand-Engine " into " the whole ileon of a cow " and laid a brick on the distal end, he concluded : " The force of the water injected protruded the Gut, and the Annular Fibres by their natural restitution promoted the motion of the water, and kept the stream from any interruption, though the Injection was made by intervals." From this experiment, " to imitate the pulse and circulation," Floyer demonstrated that with the resistance offered to the passage of blood the pumping force distends the musculature, by the contractions of which in the intervals the flow is converted from an intermittent to a continuous one.

An appendix to the second volume of the " Pulse Watch " Floyer devotes to " An Enquiry into the Nature, Use, Causes and Differences of Respiration and the Prognostication which may be made of it in Diseases." In this he recounts observations on the rate of respiration " in divers animals in a minute, by observing their breaths in Frosty Weather, or the motion of their Bellies or Nostrils." He also recorded the effect of diet, exercise, temperature, etc., on the rate of respiration and pulse as well as " the proportion of Pulses and Respirations in some Diseases." He seems therefore to have been the first to count both the pulse and the respirations by the minute.

Floyer's most important work on the respiratory system was, however, contained in " A Treatise of the Asthma," the first edition of which was published in 1698. In Floyer's day the term "asthma" was used in a vague sense and meant little more than difficulty of breathing. Floyer's merit lies in the successful efforts he made to separate various conditions included under this term. Especially he first enunciated the theory that spasmodic asthma is due to constriction of the bronchi. He also, in a dissection of "a broken-winded mare," described for the first time emphysematous change in the lung.

Floyer wrote on other subjects, especially on cold bathing. John Floyer's "History of Cold Bathing" was dedicated to The Right Worshipful the Royal College of Physicians, and is dated from Lichfield September 28th, 1702. It reintroduced the practice into England and is the beginning of hydrotherapy and spa treatment. By 1732 the book had reached a sixth edition and was being used for advertising purposes by Dr. Edward Baynard; but the observations mentioned above on the circulation and respiration constitute his chief claims to remembrance. Surely one who did such original and pioneer work on the rate of the pulse and respiration, on blood volume, on the functions of the arterioles, and who first ascribed the difficulty of breathing in asthma to constriction of the bronchi, and first described the pathological condition of emphysema, is entitled to a place among the Masters of Medicine.

J. A. G.

IV WILLIAM CHESELDEN

(1688–1752)

SURGEON AND LITHOTOMIST

William Cheselden was born on October 19th, 1688, at Somerby, in Leicestershire, near the great British encampment of Borrow-on-the-Hill. The son of George Cheselden and Deborah, daughter of Major William Hubbert, he came of a family of wealthy graziers. He received a sound classical education, and after a short apprenticeship to Mr. Wilkes, a Leicester surgeon, at the age of fifteen became a pupil of William Cowper, the noted anatomist; soon after being bound apprentice to Mr. Ferne, surgeon and lithotomist to St. Thomas's Hospital.

He made rapid progress as a surgeon and anatomist, being admitted to the freedom and livery of the Barber Surgeons Company on December 5th, 1710, and on January 29th, obtaining the "great diploma," which entitled him to specialised practice in surgery. In 1711, at the age of twenty-three, he was already a lecturer in anatomy, giving a course consisting of thirty-five lectures four times a year. In 1714, he incurred the displeasure of the Barber Surgeons Company by dissecting the bodies of malefactors in his own house. His lectures coincided with those of the Company, and apparently were more popular, because on his promising to hold his lectures at a different time, and only with the leave of the Governors for the time being, he was excused after a reproof had been pronounced by

WILLIAM CHESELDEN
1688–1752
(*From the painting by Jno. Richardson in the Royal College of Surgeons of England*)

To face p. 24

the Master. The lectures were continued, therefore, first in his own house, and later at St. Thomas's Hospital, inaugurating the system of private teaching afterwards exploited by William and John Hunter. In 1712, he was elected a Fellow of the Royal Society.

A quotation from the *Daily Courant* of March 1721 advertising his lectures is of some interest. "A course of anatomy in which will be shown all the known mechanism of the human body, together with the Comparative Anatomy of Birds, Beasts and Fishes with the various contrivances for their different ways of life. The whole to be illustrated by Mechanical Experiments, there being a new apparatus made for this purpose. To be performed by William Cheselden, surgeon, F.R.S., and Francis Hawksbee at his house in Crane Court, Fleet Street, where subscriptions are taken in. To begin Tuesday, March 28th, at 6 in the evening.

N.B. This course being chiefly intended for gentlemen, such things only will be omitted as are neither instructive nor entertaining, and care will be taken to have nothing offensive."

In 1714 and 1715 he contested the post of surgeon to St. Thomas's without success, probably as a result of his difference with the Company, as Mead was reader in Anatomy to that body, and had great influence at the hospital; but on July 9th, 1718, he was appointed assistant surgeon, and on April 8th, 1719, one of the principal surgeons in place of William Dickinson. His stormy candidature may have influenced him in becoming one of the moving spirits in separating the Barbers and Surgeons, and organising a separate Surgeons Company, of which he became one of the first Wardens, and in 1746, Master.

He continued lecturing in Anatomy, and also turned his attention to the surgery of stone in particular, probably because his master, Ferne, was one of the surgeons specially licensed to perform this operation in the Hospital. In 1723, he published a " Treatise on the High Operation for Stone," which gave a short account of the history of lithotomy, pointing out the danger of opening the bladder by the suprapubic route, and the anatomical reasons leading to the abandonment of this useful method. The book, dedicated to Dr. Richard Mead, was, like all Cheselden's writings, brief, consisting of thirty-six pages only. Shortly afterwards he himself abandoned the operation, and adopted that by which he is best known. Although not a new conception, being first suggested by Frère Jacques, Cheselden's lateral operation for stone was virtually a new invention, and he brought it to a pitch of perfection which has never been excelled, his technique being followed in its original form until the operation was displaced by litholapaxy at the end of the last century. It was first performed on March 27th, 1727, and became famous throughout Europe, his first twenty-seven consecutive cases recovering satisfactorily. There is a tale, illustrating the kindly disposition of the man and his surgical skill, which records that, having tied up a child for lithotomy, he promised sugar-plums if the boy kept still ; and, the operation over, the little fellow immediately claimed a fulfilment of the promise.

Cheselden describes the technique of his operation as follows : " I tie the patient as for the greater apparatus, but lay him upon a blanket several doubles upon an horizontal table about three feet high, with his head only raised. I first make as long an incision as I can, cutting down between the musculus accelerator urinæ and erector penis, and by the side of the intestinum rectum. I then feel for the staff, holding down the gut all the while with one or two fingers of my left hand, and cut upon it in that part of the urethra which lies beyond the corpora cavernosa urethræ and in the prostate gland cutting from below upwards to avoid wounding the gut; and then passing the gorget very carefully in the groove of the staff into the bladder, bear the point of the gorget hard against the staff, observing all the while that they do not separate and let the gorget slip to the outside of the bladder. Then I pass the forceps into the right side of the bladder, the wound being on the left side of the perinæum; and as they pass, carefully attending to their entering the bladder, which is known by their overcoming a straitness which there will be in the place of the wound; then taking care to push them no farther, that the bladder may not be hurt I first feel for the stone with the end of them, which, having felt, I open the forceps and slide one blade underneath it and the other at top and then extract it very deliberately that it may not slip suddenly out of the forceps and that the parts of the wound may have time to stretch, taking great care not to gripe it so hard as to break it. And if I find the stone very large I again cut upon it as it is held in the forceps.

"Here I must take notice it is very convenient to have the bladder empty of urine before the operation; for if there is any quantity to flow out of the bladder at the passing of the gorget, the bladder does not contract but collapses into folds which makes it difficult to lay hold of the stone without hurting the bladder. But if the bladder is contracted it is so easy to lay hold of it that I have never been delayed one moment, unless the stone was very small. Lastly I tie the blood-vessels by the help of a crooked needle and use no other dressing than a little bit of lint besmeared with blood that it may not stick too long in the wound. And all the dressings during the cure are very slight, almost superficial, and without any bandage to retain them because that will be wetted with urine and gall the skin. At first

I keep the patient very cool to prevent bleeding and sometimes apply a rag dipt in cold water to the wound and to the genital parts, which I have found very useful in hot weather particularly. In children it is often alone sufficient to stop the bleeding and always helpful in men.

"The day before the operation I give a purge to empty the guts and never neglect to give some laxative medicine or clyster a few days after if the belly is at all tense or if they have not a natural stool. What moved me to try this way, if I may be allowed to know my own mind, was the consideration of women scarce ever dying of this operation, from which I concluded that if I could cut into the urethra beyond the corpora cavernosa urethræ the operation would be nearly as safe in men as in women.

"What success I have had in my private practice I have kept no account of because I had no intention to publish it, that not being sufficiently witnessed. Publicly in St. Thomas's Hospital I have cut two hundred and thirteen; of the first fifty only three died; of the second fifty, three; of the third fifty, eight; and of the last sixty-three, six. Several of these patients had the small-pox during their cure, some of which died but I think not more in proportion than what usually die of that distemper; these are not reckoned among those who died of the operation. The reason why so few died in the two first fifties was that at that time, few very bad cases offered; in the third, the operation being in high request, even the most aged and the most miserable cases expected to be saved by it. One of the three that died out of the one hundred and five was very ill with whooping cough; another bled to death by an artery into the bladder, it being very hot weather at that time. But this accident taught me afterwards, whenever a vessel bled that I could find, to dilate the wound with a knife till I could see it.

"If I have any reputation in this way I have earned it dearly, for no one ever endured more anxiety and sickness before an operation, yet from the time I began to operate all uneasiness ceased and if I have had better success than some others I do not impute it to more knowledge but to the happiness of mind that was never ruffled or discontented and a hand that never trembled during any operation."

In 1728, he published a paper, which attracted great attention, dealing with an operation for couching performed on a boy, thirteen years of age, who had been born blind (*Phil. Trans.*, XXXV, 447); and in the same volume an operation for treating certain forms of blindness by the production of an opening to form an artificial pupil. The latter operation probably inspired Pope when he wrote:

"I'll do what Mead and Cheselden advise
To keep these limbs, and to preserve these eyes."

Cheselden was not a prolific writer, and was very brief in everything he wrote; but, notwithstanding, he was always lucid and practical. His "Anatomy of the Human Body" was first published in 1713, and ran to thirteen editions. It was well illustrated, and although originally purely anatomical, the later editions contained many physiological and surgical observations bearing on anatomy.

From the fourth edition onwards Cheselden included with his Anatomy "A short historical account of cutting for the Stone," and the following two quotations illustrate how he enhanced his anatomical teaching by showing its application in surgical practice.

Of the superior maxilla he writes: "Part of the sides of the cavities that lie next the nose are only membranes which make the cavities like drums, perhaps to give a grave sound to the voice when we let part of it through the nose. I have seen an imposthumation (suppuration) from rotten teeth in one of these cavities, which has been cured by drawing some of the last grinding-teeth, and by making a perforation into it through their sockets. The drawing one or two of the last grinding-teeth generally, if not always, opens a passage into the Antrum, but if not or if the passage is not large enough, it may be made or enlarged with a carpenter's nail-piercer or gimblet which is as good an instrument as can be for the purpose."

The levator ani is described as two pairs of muscles. "Fistulas in Ano that are within this muscle generally run in the direction of the gut and may be laid open into the gut with great safety; but those fistulas or rather abscesses that are frequently formed on the outside of the sphincter and usually surround it, all but where this muscle is connected to the Penis, cannot be opened far into the gut without totally dividing the Sphincter which, Authors say, renders the sphincter ever after incapable of retaining the excrement. One instance of this kind I have known, but Mr. Berbeck of York, an excellent Surgeon and particularly famous for this operation, has assured me that he has often been forced to divide the Sphincter, which has made the patients unable to hold their excrements during their cure, but, the wounds being healed, they have retained them as well as ever."

His greatest work—"Osteographia"—dedicated to Queen Caroline, contained numerous beautiful plates, very accurate and of the highest artistic merit, although only a few were the work of Cheselden himself, the majority being executed by his pupils Belchier and Sharp. The text was somewhat meagre by comparison, but Cheselden's sense of humour was illustrated by the picture of a skeleton dog attacking a skeleton cat.

Cheselden gained a large surgical practice, and thus

became acquainted with many distinguished men of his day. He was an intimate friend of Pope, who has perpetuated him in the lines [p. 29] of his "Imitation of Horace," and who lodged in Cheselden's house in Queen Square, Westminster, during his (Pope's) illness. In writing to Smith, describing him, Pope said: "He is the most noted and deserving man in the whole profession of Chirurgery, and has saved the lives of thousands by his manner of cutting for the stone."

Jonathan Richardson, the artist, painted the picture of him now hanging in the Council Room of the Royal College of Surgeons in Lincoln's Inn Fields. Other notabilities included Sir Isaac Newton, whom he attended in his last illness, and Sir Hans Sloane.

He was appointed surgeon to Queen Caroline in December, 1727, but apparently, in 1731, fell out of favour at court, as he was not summoned two years later, when the Queen developed a strangulated umbilical hernia, from which she died.

In 1729, he was elected the first foreign associate of the Royal Academy of Surgery in Paris. On the formation of St. George's Hospital in 1733, he was elected one of the surgeons, resigning in 1737, and being made consulting surgeon, the vacancy thus created being filled by his nominee, David Middleton. In February, 1737, he accepted the post of surgeon to Chelsea Hospital, retiring from St. Thomas's on March 29th, 1738, at the age of fifty. While holding this appointment he instructed John Hunter in surgery during the summers of 1749 and 1750.

Although his practice was extensive, he does not seem to have amassed a fortune. It is no doubt of interest to the surgeon of to-day to learn that his fee for cutting for stone was £500. He married Miss Deborah Knight, of London, who died in 1764, and by whom he had an only daughter, Deborah Wilhelmina, who married Dr. Charles Cotes, of Woodcote, Shropshire, and died without issue.

In 1751, he had a paralytic seizure, from which he seemed to recover, but on April 10th, 1752, while at Bath, he partook too freely of ale and hot buns, and, ignoring the advice of his medical attendant, died the same day. He was buried in the grounds of Chelsea Hospital, on the north side, where his tomb may still be seen from the Royal Hospital Road.

He was without doubt one of the greatest British surgeons. A most brilliant operator, he is reputed to have performed lateral lithotomy in fifty-four seconds. Moreover, he had a true scientific outlook on his profession, and possessed an original mind. He was a practical man of many aptitudes, and is credited with the plans for the old Putney Bridge and the Surgeons' Hall in the Old Bailey. He drew up his own will, which, like all he wrote, was brief and to the point. "Being in perfect health, I write this with my own hand, and declare it to be my last will and testament. I give to my daughter, D. W. Cotes, five hundred pounds, and all the rest and residue of my estate of what kind soever to my wife, and make her full and sole executrix, administratrix and assign. Witness my hand and seal William Cheselden (l.s.) 24 March, 1749/50."

He was popular, gay and genial; kind and tender-hearted; a lover of sport, particularly boxing, at which in his youth he had been very proficient. He died in his sixty-fifth year.

His memory is perpetuated at St. Thomas's by the Cheselden Medal, a prize for the student who distinguishes himself most in an examination in anatomy and surgery.

R. H. O. B. R.

PERCIVALL POTT

1714–1788

From a painting by Joshua Reynolds in the Great Hall, St. Bartholomew's Hospital)

To face p. 33

V PERCIVALL POTT
(1714–1788)

CLINICAL SURGERY

POTT was born in the year Queen Anne died and George the First came to the throne, and he lived during one of those periodic phases of activity following great strife which mark our history. There was activity in art and architecture, literature and science, and in all branches of commerce. Isaac Newton was President of the Royal Society, Joshua Reynolds was painting his masterpieces, and a new London and a new St. Paul's had arisen out of the ashes of the Great Fire.

With the eighteenth century, medicine too was entering on a new life, upon a new physiology rising from the knowledge of the circulation of the blood and lymph, and upon a rational surgery founded on the study of human anatomy. These sciences of anatomy and physiology served surgery both directly and indirectly : directly by providing improved forms of operating, and indirectly by enlarging the field for observation and the power of inductive thought of the doctors. As we shall see, Pott took a worthy part in these activities. Coincident with this awakening of medical thought came the realisation of the layman that the old hospital buildings of London, which were the legacy from the monastic era, no longer served the needs of the people.

The two chief hospitals in London were St. Bartholomew's and St. Thomas's, but they were a jumble of old and inconvenient buildings. The enlightened governors of those days, realising their responsibilities, pulled them down and put in their place fine airy wards, the best of their kind at that day. These, however, were not enough to house the sick of rapidly growing London, and in quick succession came the foundation of Westminster Hospital, Guy's Hospital, St. George's and the Middlesex.

The surgical body politic was feeling also the divine discontent. Surgeons were no longer content to be yoked with the Barbers, and in 1745 they finally separated from the Company of Barber Surgeons, and formed themselves into the Company of Surgeons, whereby the fusion of surgery with physic into a United Medicine was once more defeated.

Such was the background of the period of Pott's life. It looked though, at first, as if he might be cramped by poverty, for his father, a scrivener in the City, died when Percivall was only three years old, leaving his family badly off. Mrs. Pott, however, was the widow of Lieut. Houblon who had been killed in action after only a few months of married life. Houblon was the son of one of the great merchant princes who founded the Bank of England and it is evident that they came to the rescue of Mrs. Pott and her daughter, Miss Houblon. With their help the boy was sent to a private school at Darenth in Kent, Joseph Wilcocks, Bishop of Rochester, acting as the Houblon almoner and paying the fees. Nothing is known of Percivall at this time, but his subsequent writings show that he acquired a good ground-work of English and the classics.

At the age of sixteen he was apprenticed to Edward Nourse, one of the two surgeons at St. Bartholomew's Hospital, for the fee of 200 guineas. At this time Nourse was busy lecturing in anatomy and surgery at his school in Aldersgate Street, and we are told that Pott was employed in dissecting the preparations for the demonstrations. Up to this time anatomy had been little studied, owing to the difficulty in obtaining subjects for dissection. It is to this opportunity of gaining an accurate knowledge of anatomy that we may attribute Pott's success. Here, as an apprentice, he acquired the habit, which endured throughout his life, of making for himself accurate observations and drawing from them deductions which enabled him to treat disease and perform operations on rational lines.

In addition to the anatomical work, no doubt Pott went round the wards with Nourse, did dressings and assisted him with the few operations which had to be done. Pott served his master for seven years, and during this time he can have received little systematic teaching, such as we understand now ; but that he used the opportunities for self-instruction to advantage is evident, for in 1736, aged twenty-two, Percivall Pott was admitted into the freedom of the Company of the Barber Surgeons, and after public examination he was given the Great Diploma " testifying his skill and empowering him to practise."

Out of his indentures, Pott apparently set up for himself in a house in Fenchurch Street, where he was joined by his mother and step-sister. In 1739 the family had removed to Bow Lane, where he lived with his mother until her death in 1746. Not much is known about this period of his life. He was a young surgeon in the city. Probably he deputised for Nourse from time to time as surgeon to the hospital. He also still helped his old master in his lectures, both in Aldersgate Street and when the lectures began to be given within the walls of the hospital, as the following notice shows. In the London *Evening Post* of October 17th, 1734, there appeared what is probably the earliest announcement of hospital lectures :

"Desiring to have no more lectures at my own house, I think it proper to advertise that I shall begin a course of Anatomy, Chirurgical Operations and Bandages, on Monday, November 11th, at St. Bartholomew's Hospital.

Ed. Nourse, Assistant Surgeon and Lithotomist to the Hospital."

A few years later the advertisement reappears with the addition of the name "Percivall Pott, Surgeon, of Bow Lane."

In 1745, aged thirty-one, Pott was elected Assistant Surgeon to St. Bartholomew's Hospital; he attained his ambition, and in 1749 he was made full surgeon. There being no tiresome regulations then about retiring age, he held that appointment until 1787, when he was seventy-five, and thus, as he used to say, he had served the hospital, man and boy, for half a century.

When he retired his health was proposed by Thomas Harley, the President, at the Annual Dinner in the Great Hall. Pott rose to reply, but overcome by emotion, sat down without saying a word. His portrait, a masterpiece by Joshua Reynolds, now hangs in the same hall. It shows a clean-shaven man, wearing a wig, clad in a beautiful plum-coloured velvet coat and lace ruffles, with knee-breeches: a most becoming dress; and Pott seems to have been partial to it; for his picture by Romney, in the Council Room of the College of Surgeons, shows him in the same coloured suit, and it is recorded that he would visit the hospital in it, and that sometimes he wore a sword.

He was a spare man in early life, not very tall, of a lively disposition, fond of talking, fond of society, and fond of his family. Good at his work, of good address, a ready writer, and a lover of humanity, he had the qualities which made for success as a surgeon.

At the beginning of Pott's apprenticeship at St. Bartholomew's the hospital occupied the present site, though the ground was put to different uses. By the time, however, that he was elected assistant surgeon in 1745, rebuilding was in active progress. Under the superintendence of Gibbs, the architect, the poor little medical buildings were being cleared away, and four blocks were being built enclosing the square, much as it is seen to-day. The first pile, including the Great Hall, was completed in 1737, and the three others were finished in 1769. So Pott started his work with advantages unknown to his predecessors, and there is little doubt that his first operations as assistant surgeon were carried out in the wards of the South Block, which has housed patients for nearly 200 years, and has only in the last few years given place to the new surgical block which is immediately behind it. It is pleasing to note that his old hospital still cherishes the memory of Percivall Pott, and has given his name to one of these new surgical wards.

The fact that Pott's name lives with us is, curiously, the result of an accident. On a frosty morning in the winter of 1756 he was riding down the Old Kent Road to visit the Lock Hospital, where he was acting as "guide." He was thrown from his horse, and sustained a compound fracture of the leg. Realising the severity of his injury, he refused to allow himself to be put into a coach, but lay on the ground till two chairmen were fetched from Westminster. Meanwhile he purchased a door, and this he had placed on the chairmen's poles, and on this improvised stretcher was carried across London Bridge to his house in Watling Street, to which he had removed from Bow Lane. His colleagues, hastily summoned, took a serious view of the case, and advised immediate amputation, to which Pott consented. But just as the instruments were being prepared, Pott's old master, Nourse, arrived and decided to try to save the limb. The treatment was successful: the projecting bone was reduced, and " the wound healed, in some measure, by the first intention." The fracture was a compound one of the tibia, and not, as is still so often said, a fracture-dislocation of the ankle-joint, which is familiarly known as Pott's fracture. But Pott had to lie up for a long time, and he made good use of his enforced leisure by writing. It was then he wrote his book on ruptures, which was his favourite, and remains as his finest work. The success of this book seems to have given him the taste for writing, and he continued writing till the end. In the introduction to this work on ruptures, Pott inveighs against the quacks, and many of his remarks remain applicable even to these days. He gives accurate observations of the anatomy of the region, and states his reasons for the congenital origin of hernia. In the museum of St. Bartholomew's Hospital is preserved a specimen of congenital hernia with a roll of paper in the sac, which tradition says was placed there by Pott. Strangulated hernia is dealt with, and stress laid on the importance of early operation for its relief, a necessity which then was not fully recognised.

In 1758, he wrote on " Fistula Lachrymalis," and in 1760 on " Head Injuries." This latter treatise Sir D'Arcy Power judges as one of the classical writings of English surgery. It is interesting also in that the cases mentioned give us an inkling of the life of the times: A girl was tossed by an ox in Smithfield; a man playing cudgels in Moorfields was stunned by a blow on his head; a man received an injury during a rescue from the press gang.

In 1768 appeared his treatise on " Fractures and Dislocations," and the treatment there propounded became the standard treatment in the country. One of the most important points made by him was the need for immediate reduction of the fracture, and that relaxation of the muscles was necessary to allow of the proper setting of the bones in alignment.

The other most important work is that dealing with curvature of the spine and lower limb palsy. He was the first to describe the complete clinical picture of what is now known as "Pott's Disease." He discusses the reasons for the associated palsy of the limbs, and offers sane ideas of treatment.

Shortly after the death of his mother in 1746, Pott married Sarah, the daughter of Robert Cruttenden, a director of the East India Company, sister to Joseph Cruttenden who afterwards defaulted when he was Clerk to the Corporation of Surgeons. His house in Bow Lane being too small for a growing family, Pott moved to a larger house in Watling Street. Here he made his name and practice. In 1769, following the Westward trend of fashionable London, he took a house in Lincoln's Inn Fields. Little is known of Pott's family life, though a hint here and there is given by Hickey in his "Memoirs," and these chiefly concern his third son, Robert, who was a wild youth, and gave his father much trouble. In 1777, his practice still growing after the retirement of Sir Cæsar Hawkins, he removed to a house in Princes Street, Hanover Square. Pott was now one of the most fashionable consulting surgeons, and he numbered among his patients David Garrick and Samuel Johnson.

After his retirement from St. Bartholomew's Hospital, Pott continued to practise, but his end was near. He caught a chill after a country journey to see a patient. He took to his bed, and was attended by the celebrated Dr. Heberden, by Dr. Francis Milman, and by his colleague Dr. Austin. Pneumonia developed, and he died on December 22nd, 1789. On the day before he died he said: "My lamp is almost extinguished. I hope it has burned for the benefit of others." He is buried near his mother in St. Mary Aldermary, where a long inscription on a marble tablet commemorates his life. The appreciation by Norman Moore is shorter and more emphatic: "He was a great man and will always be esteemed one of the first of English surgeons."

It is difficult when writing of Percivall Pott to refrain from comparing him with the other great surgeon of the eighteenth century, John Hunter. Hunter was born fourteen years after Pott, and justly attained a greater fame. Not because he was a better operator, or could offer a better opinion in a difficult case, but because he was a born researcher. Hunter at heart was a natural scientist, and a fierce flame drove him to pry into the very secrets of nature. He wanted to know all about the intimate structure and inner workings of animals, great and small. He dissected thousands of specimens, and by his indefatigable work formed the great collection which is now cared for by the Royal College of Surgeons, and what is more important still, he founded a school of surgical thought which still grows and flourishes. Pott was famous, too, but in a different way. There was room for the two types of worker, and honour enough for both. He devoted himself to the study and cure of human disease. His early training in anatomy is the key to his attainments. His method of working and thinking is obvious in all his publications. He made careful dissections of the parts he was investigating; he trained himself to make accurate observations from his dissections, and from those observations he made his deductions, and on his deductions he based his treatment and carried out his operations.

Pott was in essence the consulting surgeon. He cared for his patients and taught his students, and through his influence many advances in surgery came about. Posterity may say of him that his dying hope was realised—his light *did* burn for the benefit of others. He might have taken as his motto—" I serve."

There are many notices of the life of Pott. The first, written by his son-in-law, Sir James Earle, is incorporated in the " Collected Surgical Works of Percivall Pott." The latest life, written by a student, Mr. G. M. Lloyd, was awarded the Wix prize. I have used it freely, and can strongly recommend it. It is published in the *St. Bartholomew's Hospital Reports*, vol. lxvi. There is also an account of him with some new facts in the *Genealogists' Magazine* 1935, Vol. 7, p. 101.

G. E. G.

VI JOHN HUNTER
(1728–1793)

EXPERIMENTAL SURGERY

I WISH I could tell my readers the kind of impressions which were formed in the mind of young John Hunter as he crossed Covent Garden on a morning, somewhere about the middle of September, 1748, to find a house on the north side where his brother William had established a school of anatomy. The surroundings which he encountered were altogether new to him. He had spent his life on a farm in an upland parish in the south of Glasgow—East Kilbride [Fig. 1]—where he was born on February 13th, 1728. He was therefore in his twenty-first year on the morning we pick him up in Covent Garden : short of stature, thick set, and red haired. He is to begin the study of medicine. Did any man ever enter the profession by such a strange gateway ? He had served no apprenticeship, passed no preliminary examination ; he had been rescued from an aimless idle life by his brother William, who was his senior by ten years.

London of 1748 was a very different London from that of 1936. Round Covent Garden are now grouped some seven millions of people ; in 1748 there were only 300,000. To-day there is a university with over a dozen medical schools, mostly attached to hospitals. When Hunter came to London there was not a single medical school ; there were some private ventures, mostly of the nature of coach-

Long Calderwood, East Kilbride, the birthplace of William and John Hunter.

(From photograph kindly supplied by Margaret Brown)

To face p. 42

ing schools. The one John Hunter was to enter was of a new kind. Although only opened two years before—in 1746—it had become noted for the lectures given by William Hunter and the opportunities to be obtained there of dissecting the human body. Since Harvey's time no one had appeared in London with the training and ability of William Hunter. He was teacher and researcher. He was a very proud man, a scholar, and before John joined him had become one of the busiest consultants in London.

One point more about the Medical London of 1748. The hospital physicians and surgeons, who enjoyed the privilege of taking surgical pupils, often with a £500 premium for each, lived in the city mostly, but already there was a tendency for consultants to move westward of Covent Garden.

At the time John entered his brother's school, Mr. Simmons—a west countryman—was in charge of dissections. Under him John began to dissect, and it was soon found that he had remarkable skill with the knife. No doubt he attended his brother's lectures ; soon he had to help to get things ready in the lecture room. At first he lived with his brother ; later he lived with other pupils in rooms over the ground floor of the house, which was used as a school. No money came from home, only kind and affectionate messages from his mother, then aged sixty-five. He was dependent on his busy elder brother for food, clothes, education and pocket-money. His brother, who was in touch with the latest happenings in the scientific world on the Continent, also gave him ideas to work out. One can see that such a state of dependence must be attended by a risk of disaster, and ultimately there was an open unhealed rupture. William could never forget what his brother owed him, and presently John began to think of what he owed to himself. Hence in later years came bickerings about their respective shares in discoveries made in the dissecting room of the Covent Garden School. William proved implacable; when he died, a bachelor, in 1783, it was found he had cut his only brother, John, out of his Will.

John Hunter had to wait twenty years to obtain a hospital appointment. By a majority of votes he was elected surgeon to St. George's Hospital in 1768. Let us see how he prepared himself for this post. When the winter session of 1748–9 was over (the Covent Garden school was open only during the winter), John Hunter followed Cheselden [p. 31], the surgeon, round the wards of Chelsea Hospital. He repeated this experience in 1750, and in the summer of 1751 he attended Percivall Pott's [p. 36] lectures at Bart's. In his brother's school he was ever busy reading, not printed books, but a very much more difficult book to decipher—the book of health and disease as revealed in the dissecting room, at the post-mortem, and in the wards. We find him constantly resorting to vivisection; he helps William to unravel the structure of the placenta; he is early interested in the origin of pus, and finds that pus can be formed on unbroken surfaces. Eight men are hanged; John obtained access to their bodies, knowing that he will likely have an opportunity of studying the source of pus in cases of gonorrhœa. He found that two of the men were the subjects of the disease. He found pus in their urethras, but no break in the surface of the lining membrane. Problem after problem was investigated; he had the rarest of mental gifts—an intuition as to the right experiment or observation which had to be made to elucidate the problem in hand.

We see him in 1754, and again in 1756, getting on the path which led towards a surgical goal. He became a surgical pupil, and then a house surgeon, at St. George's Hospital. Between these times, in the summer of 1755,

JOHN HUNTER AS A YOUNG MAN

(From a portrait in the Royal College of Surgeons of England. The painter is unknown)

To face p. 44

brother William sent him to Oxford in the hope that John might have his corners rubbed off and take on a polish which the highbrows of London expected in professional men. Six weeks of Oxford were enough for John, and in good truth he was right. He saved his original genius by his timely escape.

Meantime England had entered on the Seven Years' War ; by 1759, John's health had broken down. He was the youngest of a family of ten, six of whom had died from phthisis, and John's lungs had become affected. William exerted himself on his brother's behalf, and John became a staff surgeon in the Army for two years—1761–2, seeing service in France and Portugal. While with the Army, he investigated biological problems more than he operated on wounded soldiers. Peace came at the end of 1762, and John returned to life in London.

His brother had moved his school by then, and filled John's place by a man even more remarkable than John, namely, William Hewson. On his return on half-pay, early in 1763, John took a house in Golden Square and opened a school, which provided him with research rather than with pupils. Few patients asked his advice. He soon, in 1764, bought two acres of land at a place called " Earl's Court, near the village of Brompton," two miles from London. He built a small house there, with sheds and other accommodation for animals. At first the place was rated at £15 per annum, but he kept adding land and more accommodation until the annual valuation mounted up to £89. Earl's Court became the busiest centre of biological research in all Europe.

And so the crowded bachelor years slip by until we come to 1768. William then moves out of his house, 42 Jermyn Street, just to the south of Piccadilly, and John takes a lease of it. He goes to Surgeons' Hall, and passes his examination for the diploma of the Corporation of Surgeons. He was thus making preparations for an expected vacancy in the surgical staff of St. George's Hospital. As we have seen, he was elected after having spent twenty years preparing himself for this post. In the previous year, 1767, another honour had fallen to him; his scientific merits were recognised by election to the Royal Society.

I have said that John Hunter had a genius in devising experiments. Unfortunately, he made his own body the subject of one which was of too costly a nature. He proposed to demonstrate that those who held that syphilis and gonorrhœa were manifestations of the same disease were in error. He inoculated himself with what was supposed to be only gonorrhœal pus; it produced a hard chancre, a "Hunterian Chancre." Hunter played with the disease, keeping it under control with the use of mercury. In 1770 he counted himself cured; in 1771 he married a highly-gifted lady, Anne Home. She was twenty-nine, and he was forty-three. They had four children, two of whom lived and married, but neither left any progeny.

In his early married life, Hunter made about £1,000 a year. He took pupils, one of the first being Edward Jenner, whose life is told here by Sir Buckston Browne [p. 64]. Hunter's great ability became more and more recognised, and his income kept mounting until it became £5,000 a year—equivalent to £15,000 to-day.

John devoted his public lectures to surgery. Popular lecturers at that time had classes of 150 or more. John's usual number was about a dozen; each paid four guineas for a course of lectures. Of the twelve who listened to him, not more than two or three really understood his teaching, for what they were listening to was teaching which was more than a century ahead of its due season.

Both the Hunters followed a custom of the time, namely,

JOHN HUNTER
1728–1793

(*From the portrait painted by Joshua Reynolds in 1787 in the Royal College of Surgeons of England*)

To face p. 46

that of making and preserving spirit preparations to illustrate their discoveries. Thus it came about by the year 1783, Hunter being then fifty-five years of age and with only ten more years to live, that the inhabitants of 42 Jermyn Street were becoming squeezed into the street by the accumulation of Hunter's specimens. A new home had to be found; Hunter took a twenty-four-year lease of premises with a rear in what was then Castle Street (now Charing Cross Road), and a front on Leicester Square, just to the south side of what is now the Alhambra. There he spent £3,000 in building lecture and dissecting rooms and a museum. The household moved into its new home in 1785. Hunter continued to prosper in everything except health. In 1773 he suffered from a sudden attack which threatened his life; almost certainly, as Dr. J. A. Ryle has recently demonstrated, this illness was due to a coronary thrombosis. He became a martyr to anginal attacks, but struggled valiantly with his practice and his research in town and at Earl's Court. His financial liabilities became enormous; he had between forty and fifty people in his employ. He became head of the Army Medical Service of his time, which brought him pay and honour and patronage. Patients flocked to him, yet in 1790, three years before his death, we find him embarrassed for lack of ready money. When the crash came, on October 16th, 1793, his affairs were such that Mrs. Hunter and her daughter had to seek a modest lodging in Brighton, while Hunter's nephew, Matthew Baillie, and his brother-in-law, Everard Home, took steps to dispose of the museum on which John had lavished his purse and his genius. Six years after his death, that is in 1799, they succeeded in selling the contents of the museum to the Government of the time—then at grips with France—for £15,000. The collection was entrusted to the Corporation of Surgeons, which, as an acquittal of the liability it had undertaken, was given a new Charter and a new name —the College of Surgeons of England.

What did Hunter do for medicine that we should continue to be mindful of him? Great men, as a rule, are so easily labelled—Jenner, Hunter's pupil, discovered the efficacy of vaccination; Charles Bell demonstrated the action of spinal nerves; Marshall Hall discovered reflex action; Lister, antiseptic surgery. In not one of these cases is the label adequate, but the public demands that its great men should be ticketed. There is no tag for John Hunter; to do him justice we must give him a hundred.

It has been said that Hunter was the founder of scientific surgery. If by this is meant that surgery will become a science only when all the secrets of life have been revealed and mastered, then Hunter has a just right to such a title. For the obsession of his life was the discovery of the mechanism of living matter; he perceived that life was the same in all its forms; an organised blood clot in a patient in St. George's Hospital was for him the same thing as the hydra which he grew in his vivarium at Earl's Court. He applied the same method of study to both. He knew nothing of oxygen, oxidation or of the chemical nature of combustion, but he measured the "amount of life" by the "vital" heat generated, using the most delicate thermometer obtainable, to give him a standard for comparison. He knew nothing of those living units we now call cells or corpuscles; he measured the processes of "simple life" in the mass. He subjected it to all degrees of temperature and noted its reactions.

In this way Hunter tried to get at the secrets of that reaction of living matter which is called inflammation. He used his thermometer to tell him what was happening in the hibernating hedgehog, his beehives in winter, and the trees of his garden when frost was deep in the ground.

He realised to the full that if we are to understand life we must first study growth, and that of all the tissues of the animal body, bone was the one which best lent itself to an exact enquiry. He carried out an experimental study extending over many years of the growth of bones in fowls, pigs, asses, and deer; he used the modern method of vital staining and of experimental operation. He regarded antlers as bony tumours; he sought to understand how Nature produced them and particularly he desired to discover the secrets of the bloodless operation by which she removed them annually—without fee.

Living matter, by itself, had mastered the art of healing; if men were to become surgeons they must learn their art by studying the surgical ways of living matter. That was Hunter's message to his day and generation; for this reason he turned experimental embryologist, experimental physiologist, experimental botanist, experimental zoologist, experimental pathologist and experimental surgeon. What he did and what he thought can never cease to be a source of inspiration to those who enquire at first hand, for the problems he tried to solve are still those which face us—the basal problems of life.

Why, then, do the younger surgeons of to-day neglect Hunter or brush him aside as out-of-date? It is because of the unbounded success of Lister's discovery; the Listerian revolution has led them to concentrate their whole attention on the cleanliness of their wounds and the technique of their operations. Their attention is occupied with the organisms which may invade wounds and they forget a fact ever present in Hunter's mind—that the powers of healing are resident in the living flesh. No one who notes what is happening now in the most progressive lines of biological enquiry—experimental embryology and experimental biology, as represented by tissue culture, tumour grafting, transplanting of living organs and parts—can fail to see that after a century and a half we are again returning to the Hunterian outlook and the Hunterian methods of approach.

Hunter's published works are contained in six volumes—the four volumes which are included in Palmer's edition (1837) and the two precious volumes of "Essays and Observations" published by Sir Richard Owen in 1861. A study of these volumes shows how dangerous it is to say wherein Hunter was wrong or mistaken; he made many grave errors of inference—none of observation. But in the majority of instances time has proved that it was not Hunter who was in the wrong, but his editors.

There is one aspect of Hunter's life which his annotators have refused to mention, or if they have alluded to it, explained it as an aberration of a great mind. The truth is that Hunter's enquiries had made him a pagan; he could not harmonise what he found in the realms of Nature with what his enquiries revealed to his own eyes. He silently and resolutely thought and wrote as if the book of Genesis had never been in existence. The last paper he ever penned was "Observations on the Fossil Bones presented to the Royal Society by His Most Serene Highness the Margrave of Anspach." In this paper the Council of the Royal Society was alarmed to find that Hunter, in order to explain certain changes, postulated "thousands of *centuries*" and ultimately succeeded in getting the estimate reduced to thousands of *years*, thus bringing the estimate within the limits of Biblical chronology. In the meantime Hunter died, and his brother-in-law, Sir Everard Home, readily sanctioned the desired change. Even Sir Richard Owen in 1861 is an apologist for Hunter's heretical beliefs. In the "advertisement" to "Essays and Observations" he wrote: "Some may wish that the world had never known that Hunter thought so differently on some subjects from what they believed, and would have desired him to think. But he has chosen to leave a record of his thoughts and, under the circumstances in which that record has come into my hands, I have felt myself bound to add it to the common intellectual property of mankind."

There would have been no record left if Sir Everard Home had had his way. That any record was left at all of Hunter's real thoughts is due to Owen's father-in-law, William Clift. Home burned Hunter's original manuscripts, the usual explanation being that he had pilfered from them. A close study of the conventional character of Sir Everard Home and of the circumstances which surround this infamous act of vandalism have convinced me that the accepted explanation is not the true one. Home shared implicitly in the religious beliefs of his time and never doubted that by destroying all evidence of Hunter's heretical convictions he was performing an act of piety on behalf of the world in general and for the memory of his brother-in-law in particular. The world has still much to learn from John Hunter.

There are two accounts of Hunter, which I commend to my readers: one was given by Buckle in 1857, when he wrote "The History of Civilisation in England," the other is that given by Mr. Morley Roberts in a lecture to the Hunterian Society five years ago.[1]

A. K.

[1] "John Hunter and Evolution."—MEDICAL PRESS AND CIRCULAR, 1929, May 29, June 5, 12.

VII JOHN COAKLEY LETTSOM (1744–1815)

SUCCESSFUL QUAKER PHYSICIAN

THE previous articles in this volume will remind the reader that the atmosphere we now associate with medicine—microscopes, stethoscopes, careful nursing, clinical thermometers, sanitation, anæsthetics and antiseptics—was non-existent in the eighteenth century, when John Coakley Lettsom lived and flourished.

England was then a country mainly dependent on agriculture. Men lived grossly, drank heavily, quarrelled and fought brutally, and treated the sick poor with a callousness that now seems impossible in the retrospect. It was into a world such as this that Lettsom was born on November 22nd, 1744, in the remote island of Little Jost Van Dykes, Tortola, in the West Indies. It was not therefore to be expected that, with such a humble origin, he should die in London, seventy-one years later, famous as the founder of three great institutions, an enormously successful practitioner, leaving a name which has been memorable ever since for multiform activities in everything associated with medical and social philanthropy.

His father was a Quaker planter, and the fact that Lettsom lived and died a member of the Society of Friends coloured and controlled the whole of his life; for it brought him into touch early with philanthropy and reform, kept him free from the politics of the time, and precluded him from all Court and civil appointments which might otherwise have

JOHN COAKLEY LETTSOM, in 1792
1744–1815
(From the portrait in the Medical Society of London)

To face p. 52

deviated his boundless energies from the cause of humanity and the welfare of the under-dog.

At the age of six he was sent to England to a Quaker school at Penketh, and at sixteen he was apprenticed to a Quaker surgeon-apothecary practising at Settle, Yorkshire. By the deed of his apprenticeship he agreed that " he his master well and faithfully shall serve ; his secrets shall keep ; taverns he shall not haunt ; at dice, card tables, bowls, or any other unlawful game he shall not play " ; and in exchange Abraham Sutcliff, his master, covenanted to teach him " the art, trade, mystery and occupation of an apothecary." Lettsom was lucky in his master, for Sutcliff was a good classical scholar, and taught him the Latin so essential at that time for a physician. He also interested him in botany and geology as well as physic.

Five years was thus spent in the Yorkshire dales, until in 1766, at the age of twenty-one, he had finished his apprenticeship, and was ready to " walk the hospitals." He then came to London, taking with him an introduction from his master to the celebrated Dr. John Fothergill, then at the apex of his fame. Fothergill entered his protégé as a " surgeon's pupil " at St. Thomas's Hospital, which was then in the Borough, its site being now occupied by London Bridge Station.

Mark Akenside, the poet, was at that time one of the physicians to the hospital ; and typhus or purulent fever was then so rampant in the wards that when he did a round, he had two men preceding him with brooms to keep the patients at a respectable distance. In spite of these precautions, however, it is an historical fact that he died of typhus. Lettsom describes him as limping along on his rounds, very neat and elegant in a large white wig and long sword, and being very angry if any of the students spat on the floor when going round with him.

A year at St. Thomas's was all Lettsom could afford, and to get the money to start practice he had to return to the West Indies to rescue what remained of his patrimony after the death of his father.

Accordingly he returned to Tortola in 1767, but when he got there he found that all that was left of his property consisted of a few slaves. Now Fothergill had taught him that slavery was an abominable thing, long before the rest of the world, or even the Quakers, had become conscious of its enormity; and Lettsom, therefore, with a gesture, typically Lettsomian, immediately gave these slaves of his their freedom. This left him penniless at twenty-three, and completely annulled the whole object of his journey out to Tortola, which had been to raise the money to start in practice.

It was a very courageous, indeed, foolhardy, thing to do; but Lettsom never regretted it, although in later years he came to the conclusion that slaves should be freed gradually by a process of buying themselves out. Money, however, came easily to him all his life; he gave it away, too, as easily; and so now, nothing daunted, he started immediately to retrieve by practice what he had lost by his quixotic act. His clientèle were the wealthy planters and their slaves. Slaves were valuable property, and their health was worth paying for. Lettsom often saw fifty to a hundred slaves before breakfast; the rest of the day was devoted to their masters; and in this way it came about that in the astonishingly short time of six months he had saved two thousand pounds. Half of this he gave to his mother, and with the rest he returned to Europe.

By now he had determined to try his fortune as a physician in London, stimulated by the example of his revered master, Fothergill. To do this, however, it was necessary to rise above the humble rank of an apothecary as originally intended, and acquire a University degree in medicine. This was at that time impossible in London. He therefore betook himself to Edinburgh, and there he remained for six months under the great William Cullen (1710–1790), then at the zenith of his fame. A Quaker, of course, could not graduate either at Oxford or Cambridge, the only universities in England in the eighteenth century; and to obtain an Edinburgh degree Lettsom would have had to remain attending lectures for another eighteen months. He therefore proceeded to Leyden, where he became M.D. in 1769.

Starting in Practice

The year 1770 was a memorable one in his life, for in it he took his Licentiateship of the Royal College of Physicians; he married Ann Miers; and he founded the General Dispensary in Aldersgate Street. The first event turned him into a consultant, and gave him the right to practise in the city and seven miles around it. The second provided him with a wealthy wife, and so put him above risk of poverty. The third started him on that career which made his fame as a medical and philanthropic pioneer. For the General Dispensary inaugurated a new era in the treatment of the poor of London. Until then there had been no real treatment unless they were admitted to hospital. The great out-patient departments, which we now associate with hospitals, were practically non-existent in his time. What Lettsom really started by his system of dispensaries was out-patient clinics where the poor could be seen by men of consultant rank; and, more surprising still, where it was arranged that, if patients were too ill to attend in person, they could be treated at their own homes by the same consultants. These were new and totally unheard-of privileges, and obviously they must have been badly required, for dispensaries of this type sprang up rapidly all over London and the large provincial towns. Lettsom says there were

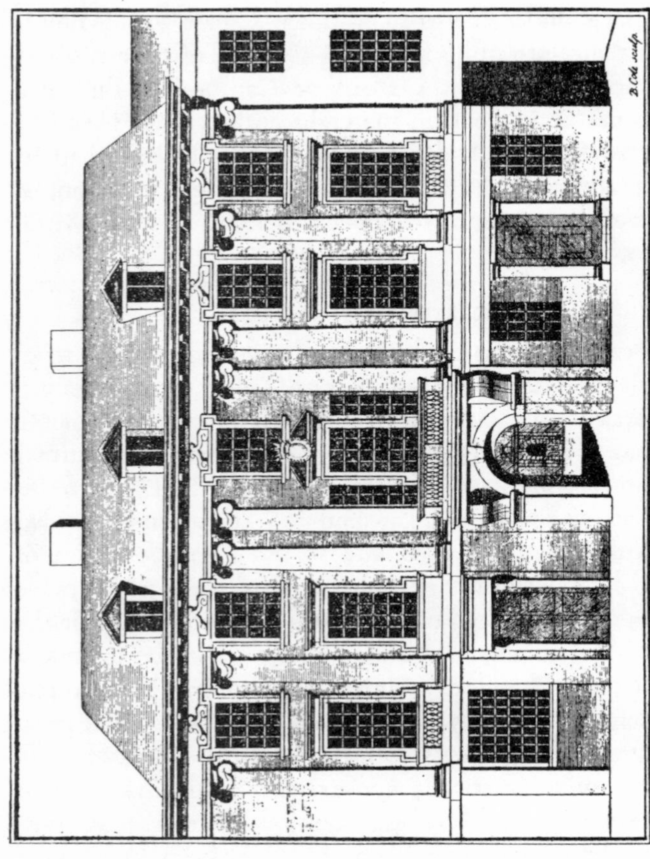

The General Dispensary, Aldersgate Street, in Lettsom's time.
(From "Lettsom, his Life and Times," by J. Johnston Abraham. London : Heinemann, 1933.)

more than forty of them by 1800. Many of them are still functioning, indicating that their usefulness is not yet over.

Obviously they were a great blessing to the poor at the time ; but Lettsom, with his quick organising mind, soon saw that they could be made invaluable for the training of medical students as well, because they provided just the sort of cases a doctor saw in after life. He therefore drew up a syllabus of lectures to be given by the staff of the dispensary, and it is one of the minor mysteries of his life that nothing came of these ideas until the very year of his death. Then suddenly and unexpectedly they fructified, for in that year (1815) the Apothecaries Act was passed, and one of the first regulations made was that "fifteen months' attendance at a dispensary will be considered evidence that the candidate for licence has passed through a sufficient course of practical medicine." This gave the dispensaries their chance against the hospitals, and for fifty years they flourished. Schools sprang up in connection with several of them. Probably the best of these was the Aldersgate School attached to Lettsom's original general dispensary, and founded by his pupil Henry Clutterbuck. Eventually, of course, the hospitals woke up to their responsibilities, and started out-patient clinical teaching. Then the schools attached to the dispensaries gradually faded away—the Westminster in Gerrard Street, Soho, being probably the last of them. Remembering these facts, one can see that it was in Lettsom's fertile brain the original idea of out-patient teaching germinated.

But his next move was more important still. This was the foundation of the Medical Society of London in 1773. He was in his twenty-ninth year when he started the Society, and it is due to his fostering care in the first forty years of its existence that it survives until to-day. There were several professional clubs and societies already in London in 1773, but they all had the drawback of being little cliques, and they all died with their founders. Lettsom's society alone has lasted from that day to this, and its long life is largely due to the fact that he built it on a broad foundation. The original rules provided that it should consist of thirty physicians, thirty surgeons and thirty apothecaries (general practitioners). To this day it has set its face against specialism in its working. It thus possesses still the unique character given it by the founder, and like Lettsom's other foundations, presently to be mentioned, goes on from strength to strength.

The Royal Humane Society was started in 1774 by Drs. Cogan and Hawes. Lettsom's name is not in the list of the original sixteen founders who met on April 18th, 1774, but he was at the first general meeting on May 11th, and they put him at once on the Committee. Thus began an association which was to last until his death. Started from such a humble beginning, the Royal Humane Society has flourished for 160 years, and its usefulness has never been greater than to-day. It speaks now to a converted world; but in Lettsom's time this was not so. Indeed, its name excited ridicule rather than patronage, for most people thought that it was quite impossible to revive the apparently drowned. Many of the rules of the Society formulated in 1774 are still in use; but one deservedly has fallen into desuetude. This was that whilst artificial respiration was being carried on by one operator, another should insert a bellows up the victim's anus, and inflate the large intestine with tobacco smoke. Lettsom was always opposed to this tobacco stimulation, and in his protests he had the support of John Hunter; but he could not get the rule rescinded until after the death of Dr. Hawes, in 1808, when he was able to issue the annual reports himself, and modify the rules to his liking. All his life he was actively interested in the progress of the Society. He wrote continually in its favour, especially when it was being ridiculed. He supervised its finances. He compiled its reports for years, and organised the annual dinner and the procession round the room after dinner of those "who had been raised from

Propaganda picture painted for the Royal Humane Society in 1787. Dr. Hawes is seated on the bed. Dr. Lettsom is standing erect with outstretched arm.

(From " Lettsom, his Life and Times," by J. Johnston Abraham. London : Heinemann, 1933.)

To face p. 58

the dead" by the efforts of the Society—a very clever piece of advertising which even to-day it would be hard to beat.

Prison Reform was another of Lettsom's protean activities. He discovered when he came on the staff of the general dispensary that the debtors in the Wood Street Compter had no doctor, nor any means of getting one when they were ill, and volunteered at once to act in that capacity. This, and his friendship with Howard and Neild, kept him continually in the forefront of prison reform. It is impossible to understand in these days how any Christian country could have permitted the atrocities of the eighteenth-century penal system. Lettsom threw himself wholeheartedly into the fight for reform after he had been called in to Newgate to attend the notorious Lord George Gordon when dying of typhus there. He was responsible for the erection of the statue of Howard now in St. Paul's Cathedral; and when Neild published his famous "Seventy-Seven Letters" on "Prison Visitations" in the *Gentleman's Magazine* [1803, iv, 1103; to 1813, ii, 437] it was Lettsom who edited and prefaced all these visitations in a series of seventy-seven letters extending over ten years. These created a furore. Neild was sensible that it was Lettsom's name and Lettsom's prefaces that made his visitations read. Many of the prisons they visited together, and the general effect of Lettsom's letters was most striking. "More," said Neild, "than I have in thirty years been able to effect has been brought about in twelve months. The gaolers are all on the alert, and for fear of being visited are in constant preparation."

Thalassotherapy and Heliotherapy, two forms of nature cure known to Hippocrates, and practised for centuries by the ancient Greek physicians, had been totally forgotten by Christian Europe, until they were revived in the England of the eighteenth century by Richard Russell, *inventeur de la mer*.

Great Britain, it will be remembered, all through that period was constantly becoming involved in Continental wars, and wealthy invalids in consequence had to be content to go to Bath, Tunbridge Wells, Bristol and other inland spas for their cures. All such places were crowded in the season ; accommodation was bad, and prices were exorbitant. But there seemed no way of avoiding the inevitable.

And then Richard Russell (" Sea Water Russell ") published his book on sea-bathing, sea water and sunshine as sovereign remedies against diseases of the glands, especially " The Scurvy, Jaundice, King's Evil, Leprosy and Glandular Consumption." It was a new thought. The sea was all round England. Anyone could get there without a fatiguing journey. One need not be wealthy to enjoy its benefits.

The health value of the summer holiday by the sea is now such an accepted fact in English life that it is difficult to remember it was unknown until the reign of George II.

Russell's book, published in 1750, started a new idea which gradually gained momentum until George III was sent to Weymouth to recover after one of his attacks of illness. It then became a craze, and the whole fashionable world

> " Rushed coastwards to be cured, like tongues,
> By dipping into brine."

Lettsom, with his intense philanthropic urge, thought that the benefits which the rich were deriving from this new treatment ought to be shared by the poor. Sending individual children down to the seaside without any medical supervision, he saw, was obviously neither safe, nor was it possible on a sufficiently large scale. And so he suddenly thought : " Why not have a hospital ? " He talked it over with his friends ; gathered a few enthusiasts around him ; summoned a meeting ; and that was how the Royal Sea-Bathing Hospital at Margate was founded in 1791. No one has as yet stressed the originality of this idea. It was the first hospital in the modern world for Thalassotherapy and Heliotherapy, and it set an example to all Europe. Lettsom, of course, built better then he knew, for it was the sun and air more than the sea-bathing that produced such marvellous cures in scrofula. But none the less, to him belongs the credit of being *the father of all the present-day open-air sanatoria throughout the world.*

It has been said that although he wrote and talked on every conceivable medical subject, he left no original contribution to science except his description of peripheral neuritis in chronic alcoholism. That is an introvert view of his life and character, and Lettsom was essentially an extravert. His mind was intensely active ; his body was never at rest. He was emphatically a man of his time, and he had the alertness to seize upon anything in his time which could possibly be put to the benefit of mankind.

Typhus and smallpox were the pests of the eighteenth century. In the first he recommended fresh air, sunshine and cleanliness. Had his recommendations been followed we should have got rid of the disease a century earlier. Smallpox is indissolubly associated with the name of Jenner [p. 64] ; but his fame and his success were largely secured to him by the advocacy of Lettsom. When Pearson tried to steal the credit from Jenner, and nearly succeeded, it was Lettsom who frustrated him. The Royal Jennerian Society was inaugurated by Lettsom. When the anti-vaccinationists, Moseley, Rowley and Birch, attacked Jenner, it was Lettsom who counter-attacked in the press ; and Jenner's grants from Parliament were secured mainly on the arguments advanced in Lettsom's pamphlet on vaccination.

All the while he was engaged in his multiform medical activities he was pouring out tracts, which he called " hints," on every imaginable subject connected with philanthropy and reform. He was also experimenting in agriculture and horticulture—we owe mangel wurzel and sea kale as food products to his enthusiasm. Incidentally these activities kept him well in the public eye, so much so that his enemies said that that was the main reason for his actions. Whatever truth there be in this—and Lettsom certainly loved the limelight—the fact remains that he made an enormous income from practice—as much as £12,000 a year in 1800, equal to £30,000 now.

But, on the other hand, it can be said that no matter how quickly he made money, he gave it away still more quickly in charity ; so much so, that about 1810 he became financially embarrassed, and had to sell his beloved villa in Camberwell Grove, his museum and library and the gardens on which he had spent so many thousands of pounds.

Incidentally, he suffered much from family afflictions, his favourite son dying tragically in 1800. But his life was not to end on a plaintive note. He recovered his financial position. He was left a huge legacy of £10,000 a year in 1812, and he continued in active practice right up to the last, dying from the results of a post-mortem streptococcal infection, a not unfitting end for one who had given his whole life to the service of mankind.

With him ended that fragrant old-world line of Quaker doctors, wearing the simple costume of their sect in the midst of the scented, powdered world of the Regency, clean-mouthed, clean-living, sober, kindly. Little wonder patients loved them, and relied upon them. Little wonder they were successful.

No sketch of Lettsom, however meagre, would be complete without reference to the epigram about him :

When any sick to me apply,
I physics, bleeds and sweats 'em.
If after that they choose to die,
Why, verily !

—I. LETTSOM.

There is no doubt it has kept his memory green when greater things might have been forgotten.

But his real memorials are the Public Dispensaries of England, the Medical Society of London, the Royal Humane Society, and the Royal Sea-Bathing Hospital.

It is enough to put him amongst the British Masters of Medicine.

J. J. A.

VIII EDWARD JENNER
(1749–1823)

It is well-nigh impossible for those living in all the security of the twentieth century, obtained for us by the genius of two Englishmen, Jenner and Lister, fully to realise the horrors of that foul and cruel disease, Smallpox. It was never more rife in England than in the eighteenth century; it yearly killed its thousands, and those who recovered were usually disfigured facially for life, and frequently blinded. George Canning (1770–1827), in one of his speeches, said: "Everyone must sooner or later expect to have the smallpox." The disease attacked the high and the low; it appeared in the palace and the hovel.

In 1744, Louis XV of France, at thirty-four, died of smallpox; many previous occupants of the French throne had died of the disease. The pathetic disfigurement of beautiful women by smallpox is dwelt upon by Thackeray in "Esmond," and by Dickens in "Bleak House." While in the "Heart of Midlothian," published in 1818, describing a scene happening in 1736, Sir Walter Scott makes special reference to Edward Jenner in eloquent terms. Jeanie Deans has walked to London from Scotland to plead for the life of her sister Effie. The Duke of Argyll drives her to Richmond, and introduces her to Queen Caroline (1683–1737), wife of George II. Scott writes that the Queen's features were good, but disfigured by the smallpox, "that venomous scourge which each village Æsculapius (thanks to Jenner) can now tame as easily as their tutelary deity subdued her

EDWARD JENNER
1749–1823
(*From the portrait by James Northcote, in the National Portrait Gallery*)

To face p. 64

Bronze statue by W. Calder Marshall, R.A., in Kensington Gardens.

To face p. 65

Python." To-day a medical man may pass a long lifetime, and never meet with a case of smallpox, and this is entirely due to the curiosity, thought, experiment and patient determination of a modest unassuming country doctor, Edward Jenner, with nothing to assist him save his simple surgery and the farmsteads around him.

His portrait painted in middle life—in 1803—by that distinguished artist, James Northcote (1746–1831), hangs in Room 30 in our National Portrait Gallery. Here we see him clean shaven, wearing his own white hair, with clear blue eyes looking at the spectator, seated at a table, his head resting on his left hand, his well-formed right hand holding a quill pen carelessly hanging by his side. On the table are shown an inkstand, an anatomical specimen in a bottle, a hoof, and the epoch-making book : "An Inquiry into the Cause and Effects of Variolæ Vaccinæ, a Disease discovered in some of the Western Counties of England, particularly Glostershire, and known by the name of Cow-pox." The book is a quarto of seventy-five pages, and twenty-three cases are described to prove that "The cowpox protects the human constitution from the infection of smallpox." It is illustrated, one coloured plate showing the cowpoxed hand of the milkmaid, Sarah Nelmes, from which the first successful case of vaccination was derived. In Northcote's painting the book lies open, with the picture of a cow encircled by a snake, the tail of the snake being in the cow's mouth.

In London, Jenner is also represented by a statue in bronze by W. Calder Marshall, R.A., 1838. It was erected in Trafalgar Square in 1858 but in 1862 (Heaven only knows why !) was removed to the seclusion of Kensington Gardens, on the eastern side of the upper end of the Serpentine. Here, as in the portrait, Jenner is seated. He wears a gown, knee-breeches and buckled shoes. The head rests on the left hand, the right hand holds a scroll and rests on the right knee. On each side of the chair appear the staff of Æsculapius and the fore part of a cow's head.

At home, in the country, Jenner appeared as a clean-shaven, good-looking man of medium height, wearing a broad-brimmed hat, his white hair gathered into what was then called "a club." He wore a blue coat with gilt buttons, buckskin breeches, well-polished jockey boots with handsome silver spurs, and he carried a silver-banded riding whip. He generally rode a white horse, and altogether made an attractive, smart and cheery figure.

Edward Jenner was born on May 17th, 1749, in the Gloucestershire village of Berkeley. He came of sound English clerical stock. He went to the Grammar School in Cirencester, and when about sixteen was apprenticed to Mr. Ludlow, a surgeon at Sodbury, near Bristol. The boy was devoted to natural history from his childhood, particularly to geology and ornithology, and specially studied the strange habits of the cuckoo and the marvellous transmigration of birds. He loved his flute and his violin. He was not averse to good society and moderate conviviality. His friends thought that had he cared, he might have become a distinguished poet, for he wrote good verse and songs, and often sang the latter. His main characteristic, however, and the secret of the magnificent achievement of his life, was his insatiable curiosity—his inquisitiveness; for, like Queen Esther, he must know "what it was and why it was." Curiosity is a supreme quality, and together with Hunger and Love, has probably led, as nothing else has done, to Man's progress on this planet. Jane Austen, with a woman's instinct, wishing to pour scorn upon the head of one of her characters—Mr. Price, Fanny's father—says "he had no curiosity." It was doubtless this curiosity, a determination to know all there was to know about his profession, which, when he was twenty-one and at the end of his apprenticeship, brought Jenner to London, where he lived for two years as a house pupil of that great surgeon and pioneer, John Hunter (1728–1793). In John Hunter he met a man of equal curiosity, his senior by twenty-one years, and a man after his own heart. A life-long friendship ensued and correspondence never ceased. For years Hunter obtained from Jenner biological specimens of all kinds, such as birds' nests, cuckoos, hedgehogs, eels and salmon spawn—a complete list would be a long one. Hunter was so much attached that he wished Jenner to settle down with him in London, but Jenner preferred the country. It was to Jenner that Hunter gave that immortal advice with regard to biological investigation: "Don't think, but try; be patient, be accurate." Unhappily, when in 1798 Jenner came to London with his great discovery of vaccination, the "dear man"—as Jenner always called Hunter—was dead, and could not enjoy his pupil's success, and give him the support he sadly needed at first.

During Edward Jenner's apprenticeship at Sodbury between his sixteenth and twentieth years, something great happened in the commonplace little surgery: something which was to benefit the whole world and to immortalise the boy. Opportunity stepped in, that mysterious something which, forelock in front and bald behind, visits most men sooner or later, but is so seldom seen, so seldom realised, until too late. "For what is opportunity?" as George Eliot finely says. "To the man who cannot use it, it is like an unfecundated egg, which the waves of time wash away into nonentity." But Edward Jenner realised his opportunity, seized it by the forelock, and never loosened his hold for twenty-five years. Opportunity came into the little room in the shape of a dairymaid. Conversation turned upon smallpox, and the girl said: "Oh, I shall never have smallpox, for I've had cowpox." This remark set Jenner thinking. On making enquiry, he found that the girl's opinion was universally held in all the dairy farms round about; but the idea was laughed to scorn by all the local medical men, for they frequently came across smallpox in cases said previously to have had cowpox. Jenner, however, was greatly impressed, and determined to prove the girl's statement to be true or false by patient observation and experiment. All was not so simple as it may have looked at first sight. Jenner soon found that there were many affections of the cow's teats and udder communicable to the milker's hand; that many cases of so-called cowpox were spurious, that cowpox was comparatively rare, and that it was these facts that had led his local medical brothers to give no credence to the popular belief. It will easily be understood how difficult was the problem which Jenner had set himself to prove, one way or the other.

The farms were wide apart, locomotion was on horseback, and his practice as a country doctor time consuming. The question, however, never left his mind. He became so obsessed that he could often talk of nothing else, and he was threatened—let us trust only as a joke—with expulsion from one of the two rustic medical clubs to which he belonged, as an insupportable bore. The next twenty-five years of his life were devoted to the problem, and finally were crowned with complete success.

On May 14th, 1796, he successfully inoculated a healthy boy of eight, John Phipps, with cowpox from the hand of a milkmaid—Sarah Nelmes—and some eight weeks after inoculated the boy with true smallpox, without any resulting disease! Jenner continued his observations, and soon felt that he was on the right road to great achievement. For some months he went about his daily work oppressed by the knowledge that he, and he alone, possessed the secret for the prevention of smallpox, and the saving of thousands and thousands of lives yearly all over the world, and the freeing of mankind from one of the most horrible and torturing of diseases.

At last, when quite sure of his facts, and having written his little book, he armed himself with a good supply of lymph, and, with his wife and daughter, started for London on April 24th, 1798. His "dear man" John Hunter, unhappily, was dead. At first, as was only natural, he met with very great opposition. It is right that all innovations should be severely criticised before being accepted, but truth is great and will prevail. The world longed for a preventative of smallpox. Men in London gradually accepted Jenner's vaccination, and it was soon accepted all over Europe and in America. But patients and practice did not come to Jenner. Vaccination, when once explained, was such a simple thing that any medical man could undertake it. He took a fine house in Hertford Street—No. 10—still standing, and spent something like £6,000 of his own money, and all to no advantage. Parliament voted him £10,000, which he received, sadly shorn by fees and commission, and very long after it was due, and later on another £20,000. His wife was ill and dying, and they returned to Berkeley. He resumed practice, and no doubt enjoyed his great fame and reputation; but no titles, no more money came his way, and he worked on quietly to the very end, dying of apoplexy in his seventy-second year. He is buried in his father's church at Berkeley.

So passed the supreme, or shall we say one of the supreme, benefactors of the human race. One remarkable for his simplicity and directness of purpose, the Conqueror of the "venomous scourge" Smallpox, and the Father of modern preventive medicine.

It is important that the present generation should know

what smallpox is, for although vaccination is not yet compulsory, its results are so splendid, that the disease is now a rare one. Two photographs, horrible and gruesome as they are, are therefore shown, taken from Dr. John Beuzeville Byles's work on the "Diagnosis of Smallpox," with his kind permission. His personal experiences are remarkable. During the last great smallpox epidemic [1901–2] he was in charge of thousands of cases, and neither he nor his hundreds of nurses and servants contracted smallpox. All were carefully vaccinated.

The great historian Lord Macaulay was born in 1800, just two years after Jenner had published to the world his discovery that "the cowpox protects the human constitution from the infection of smallpox." Macaulay therefore knew the state of this country before and after Jenner's advent, and some forty years later wrote of smallpox:

"That disease over which science has since achieved a succession of glorious and beneficial victories, was the most terrible of all the ministers of Death. The havoc of the plague had been far more rapid, but plague has reached our shores only once or twice within living memory, and smallpox was always with us, filling the churchyard with corpses, tormenting with constant fear all those it had not stricken, leaving on those whose lives it spared the hideous traces of its powers, turning the babe into a changeling at which the mother shuddered, making the eyes and cheeks of the betrothed maiden objects of horror to the lover."

The immediate effects of vaccination, on a very small scale, in its first few years, must have been extraordinarily good, to have inspired such rhetoric!

B. B.

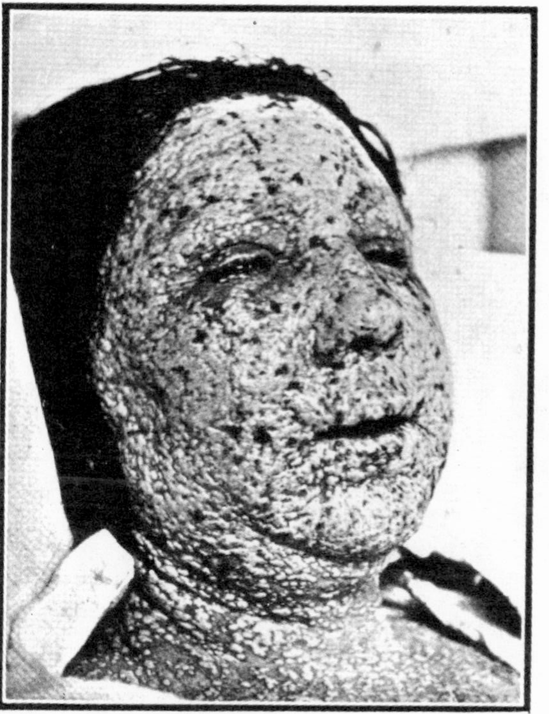

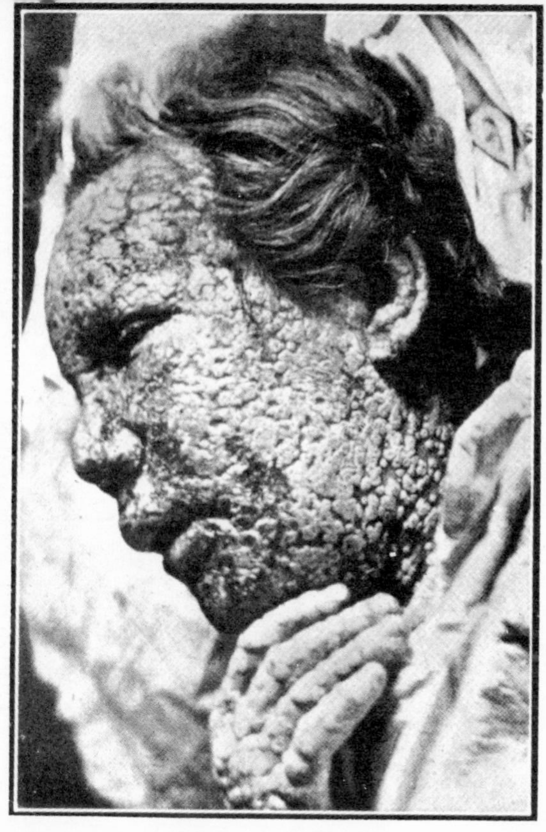

Photographs of smallpox patients.

(By permission of Mr. J. B. Byles, F.R.C.S., and Messrs. Cassell & Co.)

To face p. 70

ROBERT WILLAN, M.D., F.R.S.
1757–1812

To face p. 71

IX ROBERT WILLAN
(1757–1812)

"WE owe," Dr. Arnold Chaplin says in his Fitzpatrick lectures, "to the physicians of the age of George III an immense debt for the excellent foundations they built, often with rough and improvised tools. . . . Men of the stamp of Hunter, Baillie, Prout, and Willan, flung open the portals of medical science, through which their descendants have passed to realms of spacious and accurate knowledge." This tribute by our leading medical historian securely places Robert Willan among the masters of British medicine. And yet except to those who are interested in dermatology or in the history of our profession, Willan is hardly known. Even among dermatologists his name and accomplishments have become faded and neglected, and had it not been for the energy and endeavour of an American, the late Dr. John E. Lane, many precious records of the man himself must have been lost for ever. From Dr. Lane's scholarly essay the present writer has drawn freely: he desires here and at once to acknowledge his debt to it.

Willan was born in 1757 at Hill, near Sedbergh, where his father was in private practice as a physician. He was educated at Sedbergh School, distinguishing himself both in mathematics and classics, in the former subject under the tutelage of the Revd. Dr. Bateman. The name of Bateman is significant in this connection, and it is interesting to speculate upon the possible relationship between the Schoolmaster and Dr. Bateman, Willan's successor. We know that the father of Bateman, the dermatologist, was a country surgeon, but it would seem that there was no blood relationship between these two Batemans, or between them and Willan. Family ties had, therefore, no part in influencing Willan in the selection of his successor. Indeed, as will be seen later, Willan's first choice was James Sheridan Knowles: and, further, we know from the records of the Public Dispensary that in his first application for assistant physician in 1802 Bateman was unsuccessful—a rebuff from which Willan's influence could have saved him had Bateman then been his protégé.

In 1777 Willan began his medical studies at Edinburgh University, graduating, as was customary, three years later. There were family interests to consider, and it was intended that he should succeed to the practice of an elderly relative, one Dr. Trotter, of Darlington. Either by his own wish or counselled by his father, he interrupted the plan by a post-graduate course in London, and although he did in fact return to Darlington for a short time, and there wrote his first paper, a small tract on the sulphur waters of Croft, his imagination had been fired by the prospect of a greater career. He returned to London in 1782, there to remain to the end of his professional life.

Medicine in 1782, in its teaching and application, and in its limitations and defects, was so different from medical science as we know it to-day as to seem almost incredibly remote and deficient. Enterprising physicians lectured at their private dwellings on materia medica, physic and chemistry, and instruction in anatomy was available at the famous school in Windmill Street. We do not know whose lectures Willan attended or what instruction he received, but we do know that he became acquainted with Dr. John Fothergill, a fortunate circumstance, for it was he who persuaded Willan eventually to settle in London. Willan probably first lived in Hatton Street, for there is a letter from this address speaking of his growing business, but hazarding that there will be a little falling off "when all the doctors return from their watering places." He had now to find some public appointment, and as the existing hospitals were closed to those who were not their pupils, he had to content himself with the Public Dispensary newly opened in Carey Street, to which he was appointed the first physician in 1783. From this time his "advance in public reputation . . . was regularly progressive, though slow." In 1785 he obtained the licence of the College of Physicians. The examination was conducted in Latin, no severe test to one with Willan's classical background. Indeed, this was not enough, for he astonished the Censors by addressing them at the finish with some congratulatory Greek verses of his own making. Willan's status at the Public Dispensary was that of a general physician. The writer of this memoir some few years ago carefully searched the old Minutes for some intimation of Willan's special preoccupation; but skin diseases are never mentioned, and there is nowhere even a hint that Willan was a celebrated dermatologist. Under the master's guidance the Public Dispensary became a recognised centre for post-graduate education. Besides his successor, Bateman, he numbered among his pupils: Biett, the celebrated French dermatologist; Marcet, later physician to Guy's Hospital; and Bright [p. 79]. Addison [p. 84] was later a physician to the dispensary, and although there is no record that he was ever a pupil, it cannot be doubted that the influence of the Willan tradition and teaching led to the discovery of "Addison's keloid" and "Addison's disease."

Willan had now moved to 14 Bloomsbury Square: the house stands to-day almost unchanged. He was at his zenith and wrote (May, 1809) to his brother telling him that the family are to lodge for a part of July and August in Edgware "while the house is painted and the Grandees are out of town." Shortly before this time, about 1805, he befriended the young James Sheridan Knowles, then in dire poverty and want following a quarrel with his father. Willan took him as his pupil, prescribed his course of study, and eventually obtained for him the degree of Doctor of Medicine from Aberdeen. He intended to bestow the reversion of his practice upon his young pupil. The plan failed: if the world lost a great dermatologist, it gained in exchange a great dramatist.

Bateman in his biographical memoir tells us that in 1803 Willan's private practice had grown so large that it became necessary to resign his appointment at the Public Dispensary, which he had directed for nearly twenty-one years. He continued in active practice until 1810 when his friends observed a change in his appearance: his health began to fail. From his youth he had been of a delicate constitution, pale and slender, but in spite of this he had hitherto been able to follow the exacting demands of his extensive public and private duties. An hæmoptysis now compelled him to take his condition seriously; an easier mode of life failed to stay the course of disease: pleural effusion developed, his complexion became sallow and the conjunctivæ tinged with yellow. Finally, in October 1811 and upon advice, he embarked with his family for Madeira. Willan has left us a record of this journey in a most interesting letter, which has been published by Dr. Haldin Davis—

"Dear Brother,

After the letter Mrs. Swain would send you, written from the Isle of Wight, we had two or three very rough nights and days with a very high sea . . . among twenty-six passengers in a ship where we were packed as close as the ducks and chickens in coops on the deck. The Captain certainly used us ill in this respect and starved half of us by roasting the dying poultry, supplying us with musty flour, dry biscuits and bad water, from which after we had fairly put to sea, there was no redress. We landed at Funchall, December 1st, in a most pitiable plight after fifty-three days from Blackwall. This is almost unparalleled. . . . After resting five or six days . . . I commenced a medicinal course which seems to be taking some effect . . . I am, however, better, the swelling being less and the lungs quite free. Richard is a good boy and going on very well with his Latin and French. He will give you a letter when we have settled in our cottage at Roxinha, a very pretty spot on the side of the Bay.

YOUR AFFECTIONATE BROTHER."

The temporary improvement in health was not maintained, and on the 7th April, 1812, Willan died at the age of 55.

Bateman in his biographical memoir states that he is unacquainted with the circumstances which originally drew Willan's attention to the subject of cutaneous diseases. Willan was not, be it remembered, exclusively a dermatologist: both his practice and writings ranged through the wider field of general medicine. As early as 1784 or 1785 he had begun to study the elementary forms of eruptions upon which, as he recognised, the structure of a definite nomenclature could be built. This original plan he developed in his classical work on cutaneous diseases, which was published in parts beginning in 1798, the last section of the first half being finished in 1808. He did not live to complete the work, and although the thread was taken up by Bateman, the posthumous and edited writings lost something of their quality, possibly, as we may suspect, because of differences of opinion between the executors and the successor over the ownership of Willan's unpublished plates. There was probably an earlier English edition of which all trace has been lost, for Hebra quotes from a German translation of Willan's works published at Breslau in 1799.

Willan's teaching and writing exerted a profound influence on his contemporaries, and Professor Bloch has even stated that the book secured a recognition in all European countries such as no other treatise, before or since, has achieved. Through his book Willan influenced a wide circle : there was also a smaller and more intimate group of young physicians who came under his personal tuition at a kind of post-graduate Clinical School established by him at the Public Dispensary. Many of them, such as those whose names have already been mentioned, achieved world-wide reputations. To attract intellect of such rare quality is the privilege and stamp of an outstanding personality.

In the period under consideration infectious fevers were conspicuous and made up a large part of the physicians' routine work. The Public Dispensary issued quarterly reports of the diseases under treatment which illustrate the prevailing types. In the period from May 31st to August 31st, 1812, there are recorded 137 acute diseases, including cholera twice, scarlatina once, measles sixteen times, chicken-pox twice, smallpox ten times and unclassified fever twenty times. Willan as a physician-dermatologist was peculiarly qualified to explore the field of the eruptive fevers, and his descriptions of scarlet fever, measles, chicken-pox and small-pox are full of original observations which have in many cases been credited to others. Thus, as Dr. J. D. Rolleston tells us, Willan gave an account of non-eruptive scarlet fever many years before Trousseau's independent description of *scarlatine fruste* ; and Willan seems to have been the first to describe the characteristic tachycardia, the occurrence of miliaria, and rare complications such as orchitis. And as Dr. Rolleston has also pointed out, Willan first recorded in 1801 the prodromal rash of varicella, anticipating Gintrac of Bordeaux by 58 years.

The present generation happily protected by vaccination has no conception of the ravages of smallpox before vaccination was introduced, when any woman free from pock-marks was for that reason alone considered beautiful. From the first Willan was a warm advocate of Jenner's method : indeed such was his confidence in it that, as we are told, he carried his only son, after he had been vaccinated, through the wards of the Small Pox Hospital and examined the patients with the child in his arms. In his work on vaccination inoculation published in 1806 he demanded compulsory vaccination by Act of Parliament : this was enforced forty-one years after his death.

Allusion has already been made to the Small Pox Hospital at King's Cross. Accommodation for other fevers did not exist. Willan, who was accustomed to see the distressingly insanitary conditions prevailing in the slums of St. Giles Parish, East Smithfield, and Southwark, recognised in them the breeding-ground of disease and launched the project for a " house of recovery " or fever hospital similar to those already started in Manchester, Chester and Waterford : a site was chosen in Gray's Inn Road. In spite of a letter signed by the eight eminent physicians, the plan was actively opposed on the grounds that it would prove a source of danger to the neighbourhood. The opposition was unsuccessful, and the " house of recovery " was opened in February 1802, with Willan as physician extraordinary.

Willan may, therefore, be accounted a pioneer in Public Health. He was equally insistent upon the importance of personal hygiene. He laments that the poor are " without accommodation to clear their bodies from dirt, dust, and unctuous or adhesive substances," except by the " indecent place of bathing in the New River," and advocates the establishment of cold or tepid baths for all classes, seeing that " many ladies, though accustomed to wash their hands and faces daily, neglect washing their bodies from year to year."

Willan practised in the spacious times that are depicted so vividly by Thackeray in " Vanity Fair." His house was in the neighbourhood favoured by the prosperous City merchants, indeed close to Russell Square, where the scene of the novel is unfolded and developed. Were his patients more exacting that those of the present generation ? Here is Willan's comment in a letter to his brother. " Whatever stuff they are made of," he writes, " you will at least be satisfied on my account than they are disposed to *bleed freely* and make my wheels rattle with great alacrity six months in the year."

The portrait of Willan is reproduced from the miniature hanging in the Censor's Room at the Royal College of Physicians. It was given by Miss Mary E. C. Howell, the dermatologist's great-granddaughter, with a companion portrait of his wife, on the condition that they should be hung together.

H. MacC.

Richd Bright

1789–1858

To face p. 79

X RICHARD BRIGHT

(1789–1858)

"BRIGHT'S DISEASE"

RICHARD BRIGHT was born in Bristol in 1789. He was educated at a private school in Bristol and began his medical education in Edinburgh in 1808. In the summer of 1810 he accompanied Sir George Stewart Mackenzie on an expedition to Iceland, and he engraved several of the illustrations for Sir George's account of the journey. On his return to England he took up residence at Guy's Hospital, where he studied under Babington, Currie, Astley Cooper, Cline and Travers. He took his degree of M.D. at Edinburgh in 1813 with a dissertation "De Erysipelate Contagioso." Before finally settling in London he spent two periods of several months travelling on the Continent; he described his experiences in a quarto volume illustrated with his own sketches.

Bright was elected Assistant Physician to Guy's Hospital in 1820. After seven years of hard work in the wards and post-mortem room he published the first volume of his epoch-making "Reports of Medical Cases Selected with a View of Illustrating the Symptoms and Cure of Disease by a Reference to Morbid Anatomy." The book is adorned with beautiful coloured pictures of specimens, several of which are still preserved in the Gordon Museum at Guy's Hospital. It opens with a detailed description of twenty-four cases, in which organic changes were found in the structure of the kidneys of patients who had suffered from dropsy associated with the secretion of "albuminous urine, coagulable on the application of heat." They include examples of acute hæmorrhagic nephritis, chronic nephritis with œdema, and chronic nephritis with cardiac hypertrophy. He notes the frequency of pleurisy, pericarditis and peritonitis of insidious onset, of "apoplexy" (by which he means coma), "epilepsy," and cerebral hæmorrhage. He notes the low specific gravity and diminution in the urea of the urine, and associates the latter with his discovery that the blood is often "highly impregnated with urea." He points out that there is no direct relation between the severity of the disease and the quantity of albumen. Two years later he returned to the subject in his Goulstonian Lectures, and in the first volume of the *Guy's Hospital Reports*, published in 1836, he gives a complete summary of his observations on renal disease associated with albuminuria. He refers to the occurrence of hæmaturia and of pain referred to the kidneys. He describes the cerebral manifestations : headaches, cramps, spasms, epileptiform seizures and defective vision, which appear in some cases to be caused by œdema of the arachnoid membrane. He ascribes the hypertrophy of the left ventricle to the "altered quality of blood, which so affects the minute and capillary circulation as to render greater action necessary to force blood through the distal subdivisions of the vascular system." He regards scarlet fever, intemperance and exposure to cold as the most common causes. He recognises that recovery from acute nephritis may occur, but the usual course of the disease is progressive, sometimes with periods of improvement. Bright was inclined to be too pessimistic. A physician of forty-five with severe œdema and albuminuria, who consulted him in 1849 and was told that he would not survive more than two years, retired and lived

KIDNEY IN DROPSY.

FIG. 1—External view of one of the kidneys of King, from half of which the tunic is removed, showing an advanced stage of that granulated condition of the organ which was in this case connected with the secretion of albuminous urine. Anasarca and hydrothorax accompanied the disease.

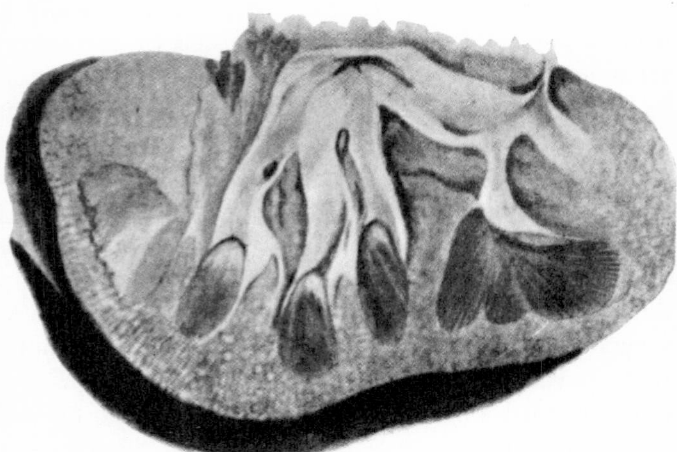

FIG. 2—A longitudinal section of the same kidney, showing the most advanced stage of the granular charge.

(Plate I of Bright's "Reports of Medical Cases.")

To face p. 81

a healthy country life, dying from cerebral hæmorrhage at the age of eighty-eight in 1892.

In less than ten years Bright had established such a clear clinical and pathological conception of the acute and chronic disease of the kidneys, which has since been associated with his name, that not much was left for later investigators to do beyond amplifying the picture by details which could only be added as a result of new methods of physical and chemical examination.

The first volume of Bright's " Medical Cases " also contains descriptions of the occurrence of ascites of long duration as a result of chronic peritonitis, the association of diabetes with cirrhosis of the pancreas, and the termination of pneumonia in suppuration and gangrene.

The second volume of " Medical Cases," published two years later, is concerned entirely with diseases of the brain, meninges and spinal cord. He describes the suppurative meningitis which may follow disease of the middle ear, nasal sinuses and erysipelas, and recognises the intimate relationship of chorea with rheumatism and pericarditis and its frequency as a sequel of sore throat. He gives a remarkable account of Jacksonian epilepsy, showing that when consciousness is retained during fits some organic irritation affecting the surface of the brain is generally found. He believes that the symptoms which arise in cerebral and spinal disease are the direct results of the lesions involving the different portions of the central nervous system, so that accurate correlation of clinical symptoms with post-mortem findings will lead to a recognition of the functions of the different parts of the brain, and predicts that the exact localisation of a lesion will ultimately be possible.

The first two volumes of the *Guy's Hospital Reports* contain numerous papers by Bright. He describes the association of carcinoma of the pancreas with the presence of liquid and floating fat in the stools in contrast with the simple fatty stools of obstructive jaundice. He had previously noted that tuberculous disease of the mesenteric glands led to engorgement of the lacteals and consequent emaciation from deficient absorption of food, but it was left to another Guy's man, Sir William Gull, to recognise that this led to a form of fatty diarrhœa, which in more recent years has been shown by Ryle to be a common cause of so-called non-tropical sprue or idiopathic steatorrhœa with anæmia.

In the same volume Bright publishes the first recorded case of acute yellow atrophy of the liver, describes the tender, swollen liver of chronic passive congestion, and the frequency of dram drinking as a cause of cirrhosis of the liver, the enlargement of which can be recognised, when accompanied by ascites, by sudden dipping of the fingers, and he points out the frequency of anæmia and a hæmorrhagic tendency in diseases of the spleen.

In 1839 appeared the "Elements of the Practice of Medicine," written in collaboration with his junior colleague, Addison. This book is chiefly remarkable for an admirable description of appendicitis, which they regard as the most common cause of suppuration in the right iliac region. The Gordon Museum contains two specimens of a perforated appendix put up by Bright.

In October, 1839, in an address to the Students' Physical Society at Guy's, which he had joined twenty-five years before, and which is still a flourishing concern, he described the clubbing of the fingers which results from empyema and chronic pulmonary suppuration.

In 1843, the last year before his resignation, two "clinical wards," Lydia and Job, with forty-two beds, now part of the surgical block, with a consulting room and laboratory attached, were set aside for the intensive study of renal disease. The results of six months' work were published by his junior colleagues, Barlow and Rees, with a preface by himself, in the *Reports* for 1843. This is, I believe, the first example of team work in medicine, and may be regarded as marking the beginning of a new era in clinical research.

After his resignation at the age of fifty-four Bright occupied his time with a very large consulting practice and with travel. He died of aortic disease in December, 1858.

On July 8, 1927, the centenary of the publication of the first volume of Bright's "Medical Cases" was celebrated at Guy's Hospital by the delivery of a Bright Memorial Oration[1] by Dr. W. S. Thayer, Emeritus Professor of Medicine at Johns Hopkins Hospital, Baltimore. The Earl of Balfour presented Bright Centenary Medals to Dr. Thayer, Professor Aschoff of Freiburg, Professor Widal of Paris, Sir John Rose Bradford, and Professor Starling, each of whom had added important contributions to our knowledge of the pathology of the kidneys, the foundation of which was so well laid by Richard Bright a hundred years before.

A. F. H.

[1] Published in the special Bright number of the *Guy's Hospital Reports*, 1927, 4th Ser., vii, pp. 253–500.

XI THOMAS ADDISON

(1793 (?)–1860)

Dr. Thomas Addison was one of the very distinguished group of physicians attached to Guy's Hospital in the earlier half of the nineteenth century. He was associated with Bright and Hodgkin, and the neurologist, Dr. Todd, and each one of this brilliant group of physicians enriched medicine by adding very definite knowledge of disease.

Thomas Addison was the son of Joseph Addison and originally came of yeoman stock from Lanercost in Cumberland. The date of his birth is obscure, in the *Medical Times and Gazette* of 1860 he is stated to have died aged 67, so it is probable he was born in April, 1793. Soon after he was born his father, who was a colliery engineer, migrated to Long Benton, Newcastle, and Addison received his early education at the Grammar School, Newcastle-on-Tyne, at the hands of Robert Stephenson, son of George Stephenson.

It is extremely disappointing that there are no records of Addison's early life as a boy and student. If these could be found they might throw light on his disposition and on some peculiarities which were not generally understood. Almost certainly he spent his boyhood studying, not mixing with his friends and fellow students, thereby retaining a shyness and nervousness which may have accounted for the fact that he married late in life a widow, Catherine Elizabeth Hauxwell, with two children. He had no children of his own.

His father prospered in his work at Newcastle, and it was

THOMAS ADDISON
1793–1860
(By kind permission of Dr. H. L. Eason, Guy's Hospital)

To face p. 84

decided to send his son to Edinburgh to take up medicine, and he went through the course and there qualified M.D. on May 1st, 1815, the subject of his inaugural thesis being "De Syphilide et Hydrargyro." After qualifying in Edinburgh, he came to London and obtained an appointment as house-physician at the Lock Hospital, and later became a pupil to Dr. Bateman at the Public Dispensary. While filling these appointments he obtained an excellent knowledge of diseases of the skin, and several of his papers and addresses are written on this subject. He immortalised his knowledge in this field by superintending the preparation of a series of wax models on cutaneous diseases which may be seen to this day in Guy's Hospital museum.

He became a licentiate of the Royal College of Physicians on December 22nd, 1818, and in 1820 he entered himself as a pupil at Guy's Hospital. It is also believed that he entered as a student at St. George's Hospital but of this there is no proof.

His merits were rapidly recognised, and his ability as a teacher of medicine earned him the post of assistant physician at Guy's Hospital, to which he succeeded in 1824. While at the hospital he was appointed lecturer on Materia Medica in 1827, and in 1837 he was elected full physician. Later he became associated with Dr. John Bright as lecturer in medicine, and in fact commenced a book on "The Practice of Medicine" of which only the first volume was completed, and this volume was largely the work of Dr. Addison.

In it is portrayed a perfect clinical picture of acute appendicitis and peritonitis, followed by a description of the morbid appearances of the disease which would pass, without criticism, except for their excellence, in any modern text-book on medicine.

Addison was the first to appreciate the epoch-making

discoveries of Laennec and the great assistance that was possible by the use of the stethoscope, and while his seniors were doubting, he boldly put into practice all the principles of the famous Frenchman, and soon became distinguished as an authority on affections of the chest.

In those days medical students paid fees for separate courses and sought throughout the metropolis for the most attractive lecturer. Dr. Addison soon obtained the best class in London, and the fees for each course could not have been much less than £700 to £800. This is a striking difference to what obtains at the present day.

Addison did not believe in specialisation in medicine. He could have been a great dermatologist or a great chest physician, but there was not one subject relating to his profession in which he was not deeply interested. He was eminently the practical physician, and this word "practical" constitutes the key to Addison's character and professional career. Addison never obtained a very large private practice because he lived almost entirely for his pupils and hospital work. He was daily in attendance in the post-mortem room up to the last two years of his life. He was never content with superficial diagnosis and always endeavoured to find a cause for the symptoms and physical signs exhibited by his patients. With regard to his character, though downright and dominant in his manner, it is said that no single instance was ever heard where a word of disparagement passed his mouth against a professional brother. The estimation in which he was held by his colleagues is shown by the fact of their subscribing to present to Guy's Hospital his marble bust. This is an admirable likeness by Towne, and is now in the Museum at the Hospital. Addison was rather a nervous man, a condition that he was accustomed to cloak by a certain abruptness or rudeness of manner. Many, though impressed by his dignity and bearing and his great moral and physical energy, found him somewhat unapproachable and haughty. During his last two years at Hospital trivial matters seemed to worry him, and he was much upset by the death of his friend Dr. Todd. He suffered from gall stones and developed jaundice, and being despondent about his health, he resigned from his office at Guy's Hospital, retired from his new house in Berkeley Square, and went to live in Brighton, where he died on June 29th, 1860. He was buried at Lanercost Abbey, Cumberland, where there is a tablet put up to his memory by his wife.

Dr. Addison's last letter, written on March 17th, 1860, is characteristic of the man. In it he says: "I can truly affirm that I ever found my best support and encouragement in the generous gratitude and affectionate attachment, and in the honourable and exemplary conduct, of my pupils at Guy's Hospital."

With regard to Addison's work in medicine, a survey of his published writings indicate his catholic interests. He wrote five papers relating to diseases of the lungs, all of them containing constructive and original conclusions deduced from the most accurate necroscopic enquiries.

In 1840 he read before the Royal Medical and Chirurgical Society a paper on the Anatomy of the Lungs pointing out that " the increase in knowledge thus acquired respecting healthy anatomy prepares us for still further advances in the investigation of changes induced by disease."

In 1837 he read a paper before the Guy's Physical Society on the Diagnosis of Pneumonia, and in 1843 before the same society a paper on Pneumonia and its Consequences. In these papers he challenged the then prevalent idea that pneumonia consisted of a pouring of the products of pneumonic inflammation into a supposed parenchyma of the lungs, and defined pneumonia as " an inflammation of the air cells of the lungs speedily producing an effusion into them of a serous-looking fluid commonly mixed with blood."

It was characteristic of Addison to seek out and unravel all problems which presented greatest difficulties ; preferring to find a pathological basis on which to build up a rational treatment rather than to interest himself in the ever-changing fashions of symptomatic alleviation.

Thus we find in 1845, as a means of throwing additional light on the origin and progress of that fatal scourge, phthisis pulmonalis, a paper read before the Guy's Physical Society on the Pathology of Phthisis ; he showed that in some cases tubercles were not present, but that bronchial dilatation and fibrosis might occur apart from invasion of the lung by tubercles. He came to regard "tubercular" in reference to what was customarily called "phthisis," as a bugbear obstructing the true and scientific explanation of chronic disorganisation of the lung.

How true his notions, based on his investigations in the dead-house, were, are apparent to us to-day when we reflect on industrial pneumonokoniosis ; how the inorganic dusts of silica, silicates and calcium and the organic dusts, both animal and vegetable, can produce bronchial dilatation and fibrosis without necessarily the presence of tubercles.

He also wrote two papers on skin diseases, one on Vitiligoidea and the other on Keloid, and both these conditions remain as obscure now as they were then.

He wrote a paper on Disorders of Females connected with Uterine irritation and described a case of Ovarian Dropsy removed by the Accidental Rupture of the Cyst.

Other papers may be found on Fatty Degeneration of the Liver, Disorders of the Brain connected with Diseased Kidneys and on the Influence of Electricity as a Remedy in Certain Convulsive and Spasmodic Diseases.

Thus we picture Addison in these days of specialisation as a chest physician, dermatologist, gynæcologist, pathologist and physio-therapeutist speaking and writing with authority on all subjects in a manner which few could emulate nowadays.

It is, however, not these able and intricate papers on which Dr. Addison's fame rests, but rather two diseases : (1) Pernicious anæmia, which he styled " idiopathic " anæmia, and (2) Morbus Addisonii, due to disease of the suprarenal capsules.

On March 15th, 1849, Addison put forward a paper at the South London Medical Society describing the condition which he labelled idiopathic anæmia, suggesting that there might be some relation between lesions of the suprarenals and this form of anæmia. It required six years of further study before Addison was able to differentiate the diseases which bear his name, and on May 1st, 1855, eighty-one years ago, he presented one of the most interesting and important of the classics of medicine on the " Constitutional and Local Effects of Disease of the Suprarenal capsules." As he said, he had from time to time met with a very remarkable form of general anæmia occurring without any discoverable cause whatever. There had been no previous loss of blood, no extensive diarrhœa, no chlorosis, no purpura, no renal symptoms, no miasmatic, glandular strumous or malignant disease. He said that while seeking in vain to throw some additional light upon this form of anæmia he stumbled upon the curious facts detailed in his paper, and states that the leading and characteristic features of the morbid state he now described were anæmia, general languor, remarkable feebleness of the heart's action, irritability of the stomach, and a peculiar change of colour of the skin occurring in connection with the diseased condition of the suprarenal capsules.

Addison published eleven cases and the pathological findings in these cases were as follows:

(1) In six cases the lesions were tuberculous, one of these leaving extensive calcification. These were Cases 1, 2, 3, 5, 6, and 9.

(2) In four cases carcinoma was found. These were Cases 7, 8, 10, and 11, secondary deposits to carcinoma of the mamma, malignant disease of the stomach, cancer of the uterus and cancer of the pleura respectively.

(3) In one case, Case 4, there was atrophy. The suprarenal capsules were exceeding small and atrophied on section giving a pale homogeneous aspect.

In neither of the last two cases was there any record of the clinical condition of the patient before death, and it seems doubtful if in any of the cases described by Addison as due to carcinoma was there sufficient evidence of the clinical syndrome that bears his name. This was also the view of Wilks who rejected the cases of Addison in which carcinoma was found claiming that they did not represent true Addison's disease. But later work has supported Addison in almost every one of his contentions. It has been shown that his view that tubercle is the usual lesion found in the suprarenals is absolutely true. Conybeare and Millis (1924) described 29 cases at Guy's Hospital. 22 of these were considered to be due to fibrocaseous tuberculosis and 6 to atrophy. At the London Hospital, the records of the Bernard Baron Institute of Pathology from 1907–1932 showed that in 30 cases of Addison's disease 21 were due to fibrocaseous tuberculosis and 9 were due to simple atrophy. Secondly it has been established that malignant processes in the glands may lead to a partial Addisonian syndrome, and lastly that anæmia in some degree, both in the characters and amount of the blood, is a definite feature of Addison's disease. The method by which Thomas Addison was enabled to separate Addisonian or pernicious anæmia from suprarenal disease was by laborious investigations of the clinical state of his patients and by accurate pathological investigation of the conditions found after death.

To his contemporaries Addison was best known as a great teacher. To us he is known as the man who first described two separate diseases, (1) Addison's anæmia and (2) Morbus Addisonii, thus fulfilling the prophecy of the writer of his obituary notice in the *Medical Times and Gazette* of 1860 where he said : " and this reminds us of this late great discovery which although of very little practical importance in connection with Addison's career as a teacher will do more than any other circumstance to perpetuate his name ; and in this again we perceive his wonderful acumen."

T. T.
&
H. R. T.

REFERENCES

" Anæmia and Diseases of the Suprarenal Capsules," *London Medical Gazette*, 1849, xliii, 517.

" Munk's Roll of Royal College of Physicians," Ed. 2, Vol. 3, p. 205.

" Constitutional and Local Effects of Disease of the Suprarenal Capsules," London 1855.

" A Collection of the Published Writings of Thomas Addison, M.D.," New Sydenham Society, Vol. xxx, 51.

Medical Times and Gazette, 1860, ii, 20.

Guy's Hospital Reports, 74, 369–75, 1924.

XII WILLIAM STOKES
(1804–1878)
CLINICAL PHYSICIAN

THE advance in medical science during the last fifty years has been so rapid and has taken place in so many directions that the present-day medical student may almost be forgiven if he is inclined to ignore or even at times forget that it is only owing to the work of those who laid securely the foundations of our knowledge that the recent advances have been possible. To-day X-ray examinations, cardiographic examinations, estimations of basal metabolism, biochemical tests and bacteriological investigations are all invoked to help in the solution of our clinical problems. But it is as true to-day as it was in the time of Hippocrates that a thorough knowledge of symptomatology is an essential preliminary to a proper understanding and weighing of the facts elucidated by the above-mentioned examinations. It is also true that careful observation at the bedside and the detection of those physical signs which are discoverable by ordinary clinical examination are equally essential. Medicine is said to rest on the tripod of anatomy, physiology and pathology, but when these three sciences are mastered the clinician must add to them a knowledge of symptomatology and a capacity for ordinary clinical examination before he can be regarded as a competent physician, and he must for ever remain thankful to those pioneers who laid securely the foundations of our art.

WILLIAM STOKES
1804–1878

To face p. 92

Amongst those pioneers the name of William Stokes is pre-eminent. William Stokes was born in Dublin in the year 1804. He was the second son of Whitley Stokes, at one time Fellow of Trinity College, Dublin, Regius Professor of Medicine, Dublin University, and Physician to the Meath Hospital. Whitley Stokes was a man of many parts : a politician in his early life, a student of the natural sciences and of the arts, and a man of broad general culture. Devoted to his family, he made companions of his sons, and especially of his second son, William, who from an early age accompanied him on many of his archæological and scientific excursions, and in consequence early acquired a taste for the observation of natural phenomena and a vivid interest in the personal observation of everything concerned with plant and animal life. Much has been witten of late on the varying importance of heredity and of environment in the development of character. Stokes was fortunate in both respects. He came of a family distinguished through many generations for its love of science. Helped by this inheritance, there is little doubt that it was the training received from his father's hands which led to the development of his latent powers and gave to the world the full measure of his genius. After studying clinical medicine for a short time in the Meath Hospital, and chemistry in the chemical laboratory of Trinity College, Stokes went, in 1823, to Glasgow, where he devoted himself for a couple of years to the study of chemistry. He then transferred himself to Edinburgh, where he came under the influence of Professor Alison, a humane and practical physician. From Alison, Stokes imbibed a profound love of clinical medicine. Under his tuition his powers of observation rapidly developed, and along with these powers there grew up in him a great love of his fellow men and a great sympathy with the sick and afflicted.

At this time the writings of Laennec were giving rise to much discussion, and the forward-looking men began to realise the importance of the new methods of diagnosis which that brilliant Frenchman advocated. Stokes immediately recognised the value of the stethoscope, and while yet a student published a small treatise which perhaps more than any other of his works has brought him persistent fame. It was entitled "On the Use of the Stethoscope." He returned to Dublin in 1825 and at once started clinical work in connection with the Dublin General Dispensary. In the following year his father resigned his position as visiting physician to the Meath Hospital, and William Stokes, already well known for his treatise on the stethoscope referred to above, had no difficulty in securing his election to the vacant position.

Now began those series of clinical lectures which soon made the Dublin School of Medicine known far and wide, and which attracted students from all over the world. Stokes had as his colleague the famous Graves. The two men worked together in perfect harmony. Both were possessed of rare enthusiasm. They reorganised the teaching of clinical medicine, making it clinical in the true sense of the word, and insisting on the importance of close, careful and continued observation of patients. But Stokes did more than teach. He also wrote. During the next twelve years and, indeed, throughout his entire life, many papers of importance appeared from his pen. These were contributed to various medical journals, but especially the *Dublin Journal of Medical Science*, of which he was editor. Then, in 1837, appeared "The Diagnosis and Treatment of Diseases of the Chest." This book, which can be read with much profit to-day, finally established Stokes' reputation as one of the greatest clinicians of his time. It is full of vivid pen pictures of disease, and contains numerous original observations. To many it brought home for the first time the importance of auscultation in the diagnosis of pulmonary disease. Following this publication he received many honours, and in 1845 was elected Regius Professor of Medicine in Dublin University in succession to his father, a post which he himself held up to the time of his death.

During the following years Stokes devoted much attention to diseases of the vascular system, and contributed many papers to scientific journals on diseases of the heart and blood vessels. These papers formed the basis of his book entitled "Diseases of the Heart and Aorta," which may be regarded as a companion volume to his book on "Diseases of the Lungs." Although at the time of its publication this book seems to have produced less impression than the former volume, there is no doubt that from the standpoint of clinical acumen it must be ranked as the more important of the two. By the time the work had appeared, the world of medicine was almost entirely occupied with the observation of physical signs. Physical signs, indeed, had been elevated into a position of much greater importance than symptomatology. There was even a tendency to neglect the history of the patient and his reactions, while ever-increasing refinement in the differentiation of signs was aimed at. Stokes, however, realised that the mere differentiation of valvular defects was of comparatively little importance as compared with a clear estimation of the condition and strength of the cardiac muscle. His teaching in this respect was not fully appreciated, for it was not till the time of Sir James Mackenzie [p. 214] that the profession as a whole began to realise the truth of what Stokes persistently emphasised. Had his precepts been followed, many a young man condemned to an invalid or valetudinarian life owing to the existence of a simple cardiac murmur would have been spared the unhappiness which such a lot produces, and would have been enabled to play his part in the service of the community. The advice Stokes gave regarding the treatment of fatty disease of the heart foreshadowed the Schott (1839–86) treatment of later days. He realised that the myocardium was a muscle, and that it must be trained like any other muscle; that too much rest and too much care, instead of doing good, would do harm; in consequence he recommended moderate activity and the abandonment of luxurious habits. In this book also is to be found a description of a case which presented the symptom since then known as Cheyne-Stokes respiration.

In 1818, John Cheyne, a physician who, born in Leith and educated in Scotland, had settled in Dublin, published in *The Dublin Hospital Reports* his observations on "Rhythmical ascending and descending periods of respiration separated from one another by short pauses." Stokes's description amplified that given by Cheyne, and, further, Stokes emphasised the serious prognostic import of the symptom.

He also recorded a case of what is now called the Stokes-Adams syndrome. In 1826 Stokes, in conjunction with Adams, published an article entitled "Essential Heart Block." In this article all the symptoms of severe recurrent heart block are described: the very slow pulse, the prolonged fainting attacks and the frequent presence of evidence of aortic disease. In his book Stokes refers to the subject, and in a vivid narrative fixes for all time the characteristic features of the malady. It remained for his successors to explain the phenomena which are described, and to prove that the cases which he referred to were only special examples of a comparatively common condition.

Twenty years later, in 1874, his great monograph on fevers was published. Although full of the wisdom of ripe experience and observation this book was, even at the time of its publication, of less value than his two previous works. It bore evidence of the conservatism which seizes even the most alert of minds and which renders them, as years go by, unwilling to modify accepted opinions, and somewhat intolerant of new ideas.

In 1878 Stokes became ill from a paralytic stroke, and passed away quietly after an illness of a couple of months' duration.

This rapid sketch of his career gives no real picture of the man himself. He was a man of indomitable energy and of wide information. His interests were not limited to his profession. Music, painting, indeed, the arts in general; travel, archæology, all attracted him, and in his home he was constantly surrounded by men of distinction in every branch of learning. His own breadth of view led him to regard the profession of medicine from a much wider outlook than was common amongst his contemporaries, and one of the great services that he rendered to medicine was his insistence on the fact that a doctor must not be trained as a mere technician, but must be thoroughly educated. In various addresses given in Trinity College, at the Meath Hospital and to the British Medical Association when he presided over the Annual Meeting of that Association in Dublin in 1867, he insisted that medical men should receive at least as good a general education as did the students for the Church or law.

At that time there was a tendency to decry the value of the Arts course for medical students in Trinity College, and since Stokes's time many attempts have been made to whittle it down or even to abolish it altogether. Fortunately, however, for the prestige of the Trinity College

Medical School, the views of Stokes, so ardently and frequently promulgated during his lifetime, have been upheld by his successors, and so it is still necessary for the medical graduate in Dublin University to obtain also a Degree in Arts. Stokes's views, however, affected a wider public, and impressed universally the importance of the training of medical students as distinct from the mere supplying them with technical knowledge. In this connection we must also refer to the high ethical standard in the profession which he always inculcated. Again and again in talking to his students and in public addresses he emphasised the importance of observing the highest and most strict professional rules of conduct. In every detail he himself provided an almost perfect example. Courteous and calm, firm of purpose, kind and reticent, he obtained the confidence of all those who consulted him, and invariably preserved the secrecy of that confidence.

With all his professional brethren he was on the best possible terms. He contended forcibly for an improvement of the status of both consultants and general practitioners, while in especial he took a leading part on behalf of the Dispensary Medical Officers in Ireland. Under the Medical Charities Act of 1851 the whole of Ireland was divided up into some eight hundred and ten dispensary areas, to each of which a doctor was appointed. The duties of dispensary doctors were manifold, and abuses were many. Before long it was realised that for the miserable salaries which were paid, an amount of work was demanded which often taxed the physical powers of a medical officer to the utmost. Into all these grievances it is unnecessary to enter. It is only within recent years that the last of them has been removed, but in the early stages of the fight Stokes played a notable part. One of his most telling arguments was the high rate of mortality amongst dispensary medical officers. The hardships which they were compelled to undergo, combined with the constant exposure to infection, rendered them particularly liable to fall victims to typhus fever. Stokes collected his figures carefully to illustrate this fact, and though in his own lifetime he saw little results from his efforts, there is not the least doubt that he helped to sow the seeds which bore fruit some fifty years afterwards. Of his other notable contributions to the advance of the medical profession it is impossible to speak in detail. In 1838 he founded the Dublin Pathological Society, a Society of which the present Royal Academy of Medicine in Ireland may be regarded as the lineal descendant. To him also was due to a large extent the establishment of a Diploma in State Medicine in Dublin University, the first Diploma of its kind in the British Isles. His practical foresight made him realise early in life that State Medicine, or as it is perhaps better called, the Public Health Services, would become more and more important, and would even within his own lifetime enter more and more into the daily life of the everyday citizen. His address to the British Medical Association in Trinity College in 1867, is prophetic in this respect, and was followed five years later by the establishment of the Diploma above referred to. This address focused the attention not merely of the profession, but also of statesmen and public men in general, on the absolute necessity of taking steps to preserve the health of the nation. Practically every one of the suggestions made in that address have been adopted, and have long since become part of the routine public health services. Stokes also realised, as did the Greeks of old, that medicine and surgery are really one, and that any artificial barrier between them was absurd and should be broken down. He pressed in season and out of season that physician and surgeon should both receive the same scientific education, and that no man should be permitted to practise medicine unless he had received training in both branches of his art. Holding these views, it was natural that he should be appointed a member of the General Medical Council when that body came into being in 1858. Throughout his life he received many distinctions, far too many to enumerate here. We can only say that his pre-eminence as a scientist was recognised by his being elected a Fellow of the Royal Society in the year 1863, perhaps the most coveted distinction in the whole world of science, and one which is comparatively seldom gained by a member of the medical profession. Stokes died in 1878, but his spirit still lives, not only in the Meath Hospital, but also as an inspiration to all clinical teachers in the Irish school.

T. G. M.

SIR WILLIAM FERGUSSON, BART., F.R.S.
1808–1877
(From the portrait, painted in 1874 by Rudolph Lehmann, in the Royal College of Surgeons of England)

To face p. 101

XIII WILLIAM FERGUSSON
(1808–1877)
OPERATIVE SURGERY

William Fergusson was the son of James Fergusson, of Lochmaben, Dumfriesshire, and was born on March 20th, 1808, at Prestonpans. His early education took place at Lochmaben, but later at the High School, Edinburgh. After leaving school at the age of fifteen he commenced to study law, and was placed in a lawyer's office at his own wish. After two years he found the work uncongenial and gave up the study of law for that of medicine, to the delight of his parents, who always had wished him to become a doctor.

Fergusson found no difficulty with his early medical studies in Edinburgh, and soon came under the observant eye of Dr. Knox, who at that time had a great reputation as an anatomist, both at home and abroad. Professor Fraser-Harris, in a communication to Sir Buckston Browne, writes :

"In the winter session, 1828–9, William Fergusson was a student of, and prosector for, Knox, in which latter capacity he seems now and again to have interviewed Burke and Hare when they arrived with 'subjects.' He is specifically named in Burke's holograph confession, a facsimile of which I gave to the Wellcome Museum years ago. The passage is : 'That worthy gentleman, Mr. Fergusson, was the only man that ever mentioned anything about the bodies. He asked where they got the girl Mary Paterson, because she would seem to have been well known to some of the students. Her body was so well formed that Knox would not allow it to be dissected, but preserved it in spirit, and called in Samuel Joseph, the artist, to make a sketch of it. Fergusson was called as a witness at the trial. His name was forty-seventh in the official list of fifty-five. "Forty-seven, William Fergusson, now lately residing in Charles Street, in or near Edinburgh, with his brother John, now or lately, writer."' "

Fergusson became a demonstrator in anatomy, and the Museum at Edinburgh still contains some very fine dissections of his. Although keen on anatomy, his main ambition was to practise surgery, and in 1828 he became a licentiate of the Edinburgh College of Surgeons, gaining the Fellowship a year later. In 1831 he was elected surgeon to the Edinburgh Royal Dispensary, and during the same year he startled the surgeons in Scotland by tying the third part of the right subclavian artery, an operation which had been performed only twice before that time. He now spent most of his time in the practice of surgery, and was an indefatigable worker. He seemed never to tire, however much work he had to do. In October, 1833, he married Miss Helen Hamilton Ranken, the daughter and heiress of William Ranken, of Spittlehaugh, Peeblesshire. Fergusson was placed in easy circumstances as a result of this marriage, but it did not have the effect of lessening his zeal for surgery: if anything, it had the opposite result. Three years after his marriage he was elected surgeon to the Royal Infirmary, Edinburgh. At this time he shared, with Professor Syme, the best surgical practice in Scotland.

Soon afterwards, in 1840, Fergusson accepted the professorship of surgery at King's College, London, which carried with it the surgeoncy at King's College Hospital.

The same year he took the conjoint final, and in 1844 became a Fellow of the Royal College of Surgeons of England. On his arrival in London, he lived at Dover Street, Piccadilly, but at a later date, in 1847, he removed to George Street, Hanover Square. It took very little time for his practice to grow in London, for his fame had already spread beforehand. King's College Hospital, although one of the newer hospitals in London at that time, had created a great reputation for itself under the influence of such men as Watson, Green, Todd [p. 110] and Partridge, and the appointment of Fergusson was a very wise one on the part of the Council of King's College. Perhaps it was the knowledge of the wisdom of this appointment which led them, some years later, to persuade Joseph Lister to take the Chair of Clinical Surgery.

When Fergusson came to London, Robert Liston was the shining light in surgery; both men were similar in many ways. They were both of powerful build, dexterous in their manipulations in surgery, quick and painstaking to a degree in their surgical technique.

Fergusson's reputation spread far and wide, not only as a brilliant operator, but on account of his being amongst the first to practise "conservative surgery." Excision of the elbow- and knee-joints for tuberculous disease were so popularised by him that many surgeons followed his example instead of performing amputation, which up to that time had been the usual procedure in these cases. At King's College Hospital it was often said that Fergusson had the eye of an eagle, the heart of a lion, and the hand of a lady. Fergusson also enjoyed a great reputation as a lithotomist. At that time a vesical calculus was always removed through the perinæum, and nearly always by lateral incision. Lateral lithotomy, perfected by Cheselden [p. 24], remained the operation for stone in the bladder until the revival of the suprapubic method about 1880. Aberdeen, Norwich and London all produced their special lithotomists, for the lateral operation was beset with many pitfalls, and called for unusual skill, determination and courage on the part of the surgeon before the use of anæsthetics.

Fergusson usually operated on Saturday afternoons at King's College Hospital, then situated just behind the Royal College of Surgeons. Sir Buckston Browne, perhaps the only living lithotomist, when a student, used to attend these Saturday operations, and he recollects Fergusson in the operating theatre as being very carefully dressed in black frock coat and black bow tie. His boots were called in those days, " Bluchers," half boots, no laces or buttons, square-toed and highly polished. The patient having been brought in, Fergusson donned a white apron and turned his voluminous white wristbands well upwards. He now stood erect, silent, watchful and expectant, gently rising and falling upon his toes and heels. When the anæsthetist had given the signal that the patient was " under," Fergusson, standing on his patient's left side, passed a large, laterally-grooved steel staff into the bladder ; contact with the stone being ascertained, he handed the staff to his assistant. The staff was held vertically, well up against the pubes. A dresser took charge of each leg, the knees and hips being completely flexed and the patient's buttocks brought well over the end of the operating table. Seated on a stool, with a few simple instruments on another stool on his right, and having ascertained that the rectum was completely empty, Fergusson adjusted the staff lightly and gently. He then quickly made a skin incision from the mid-line towards the left ischium, and with the same knife plunged in to meet the groove in the staff. It was this hitting of the staff which was often blundered, but Fergusson never failed, and one could almost hear the immediate impact of the knife with the staff. He ran the knife along the groove into the bladder, slightly lateralised its blade, and brought it out cutting down and towards the ischium. His left forefinger was passed into the bladder and the assistant told to withdraw the staff. In went the stone forceps to be opened, swept round, the stone seized and extraction slowly and carefully made. No attention whatever was paid to hæmorrhage : " tie his legs together," was all that Fergusson said, and so ended, as far as a spectator was concerned, a beautiful piece of skilled surgical mechanism ; not a moment lost, not a moment wasted. On one occasion when he was performing a lithotomy operation the blade of his knife became detached from the handle. He seized the blade in his long deft fingers, finished the operation, and said to the onlookers, " Gentlemen, you should be prepared for any emergency. . . ."

The following account of an afternoon visit to the operating theatre of King's College Hospital is taken from the *Medical Times* of Saturday, September 12th, 1840 [vol. 2, p. 289] :

" Mr. Fergusson entered the theatre, accompanied by Dr. Todd, and shortly after, the first patient, an adult female, was placed upon the table. She was labouring under a painful enlargement of the bursa, situated on the head of the tibia, which prevented her from walking. Mr. Fergusson made a perpendicular incision over the centre of the patella, through the skin, about two inches and a half in length, and had some difficulty in dissecting the cyst from the adjoining skin, to which it was closely and firmly adherent. The operation was, however, completed in two minutes, and the operator remarked, although he had often removed larger tumours, he had never met with one where the cyst was so large as in the present instance. The lips of the wound were brought together, and united by three sutures, over which was placed lint saturated with cold water. The next patient was a male child, labouring under white swelling of the knee-joint, and complete atrophy of the leg. It was impossible to save the limb. Mr. Fergusson amputated the thigh by the flap operation, immediately above the insertion of the ligamentum patellæ. The limb was removed, the vessels secured, and the wound dressed, in the space of three minutes and a half. The third patient had suffered from fistula in the perinæum for several years, in addition to which he was now labouring under a stricture of the urethra, so severe as not even to admit of the passage of the smallest-size bougie. The canal was quite obliterated near the bulb. Mr. Fergusson, having in vain attempted to pass a catheter, proceeded to cut into the urethra through the perinæum. Owing to the extreme induration of the parts, he was obliged to cut his way before him, incision by incision, until he opened the urethra; the parts would not yield before pressure of the finger, after the first incision or two, as in ordinary instances. This was one of those troublesome operations which try both the patience and temper of the operator more than others, even of greater importance. We certainly admire the coolness with which the operator bore the delay in getting into the bladder, arising from the above-mentioned causes, over which he could have no control, and were pleased with our new acquaintance. Mr. Fergusson is certainly a first-rate operator."

Fergusson's visits to his wards took place on Fridays, and the cases for operation were then selected. He exercised his powers of observation so that on his visits to the wards nothing escaped him. He would point out changes in the patient, in the arrangement of the beds, in the nurses, etc., but he did not do any systematic teaching to the students ; his visit was only a walk round and the selection of the cases upon which he would operate the following Saturday. His examination of patients in the wards was only a matter of palpation, and he never omitted to turn round and dip his fingers into a bowl of water which was in the hands of a nurse following him. He never probed wounds or prescribed drugs. He did not lecture or pretend to teach, and he left so much for his house-surgeon to do that the appointment was of great value and much sought after.

Although a poor teacher Fergusson wrote a " System of Practical Surgery " in 1842 which was popular both in this country and abroad, the fifth edition appearing in 1870. But he did not take any pains to keep himself up to date with modern medicine, and his views on pathology were distinctly antiquated. His students were always keen to recite an incident which has been handed down from one generation to another. It occurred on one of those rather rapid ward rounds when a student told Fergusson that the pathology of caries and necrosis, which he had just been describing to his class, did not agree with that of Niemeyer. " Sir," replied the great man, " Nehemiah was a gentleman who wrote one of the books of the Old Testament, but I have yet to learn that he had views on caries and necrosis."

One of Fergusson's assistants at King's College Hospital was Henry Smith, and he had ample opportunity of forming an opinion as to the character and attainments of his chief. Smith said of Fergusson that " he was a thorough gentleman in every sense of the word, considerate of others, courteous and dignified in his bearing, possessed of a rare command of temper and of great coolness and decision as a surgeon, but perhaps a little too easy-going and good-natured."

In 1849 Fergusson was appointed Surgeon-in-Ordinary to the Prince Consort, and in 1855 Surgeon-Extraordinary. In 1867 came his appointment as Serjeant-Surgeon to Queen Victoria, at which time he was the leading operator in London. He was elected to the Council of the College of Surgeons in 1861, and became President of the College in 1870. Many honours came to him, and in 1866 he was created a Baronet, and shortly afterwards some three hundred of his old pupils gave him a dinner, at which they presented him with a silver dessert service. He was a Fellow of the Royal Society, and LL.D. of Edinburgh University and President of the British Medical Association in 1873.

Fergusson spoke with a strong Scottish accent and frequently used the word "mon." In manner he was cheerful and kindly, and rarely found fault with his house-surgeon or dressers. He was given to friendly hospitality and he sometimes invited his friends to dine at the Albion Tavern. On one occasion he sent an invitation to the then Editor of *Punch*, who replied to him as follows: "Look *out* for me at seven, look *after* me at eleven.—Yours, Mark Lemon."

Fergusson died in London in 1877 from Bright's disease, and was buried at West Linton, Peeblesshire. A full-length portrait in oils hangs in the Secretary's room at the College of Surgeons of England, and an excellent plaque is to be seen in the main lecture theatre of King's College Hospital Medical School. At King's College Hospital a ward is named after him.

A short time after his death Sir James Paget in his Hunterian Oration delivered at the Royal College of Surgeons in 1877 referred to Sir William Fergusson saying: "The great master of our art, the greatest practical surgeon of our time is gone. Men will no longer watch those eyes that were so keen : nor try to imitate those hands that were so strong, and yet so sensitive, so swift and light, nor wonder at that clear and prompt invention, the perfect calmness in the greatest difficulties. All these are gone and with them are gone those things that endeared him to us still more, the warm heart, the friendliness, the generous rivalry, the social grace. These are gone, but Fergusson's lessons still remain amongst us, and among them all will be that every man according to his ability should have both art and science, should work as with both hands, as if with one mind and one design."

C. P. G. W.

XIV ROBERT BENTLEY TODD, M.D.

(1809–1860)

CLINICAL NEUROLOGIST AND CLINICAL TEACHER

Robert Bentley Todd, one of a large and well-known family, was born in Dublin on April 9th, 1809. He was the second son of Charles Todd, a distinguished surgeon of Dublin, who died at the early age of forty-four. His elder brother, the Rev. James Henthorn Todd, D.D., became Regius Professor of Hebrew at Dublin University. Bentley Todd was trained at Trinity College, Dublin, where he obtained the B.A. degree in 1829. His earlier medical education was received at Richmond Hospital, Dublin, where he was a pupil of Dr. Robert James Graves, F.R.S., distinguished both as a physiologist and as a physician, who was President of the Irish College of Physicians in 1843 and 1844.

In 1831 Bentley Todd obtained the L.R.C.S. of Dublin, and in the same year he came to London and was admitted a member of the Royal College of Surgeons. He obtained the L.R.C.P. Lond. on February 23rd, 1833. His first appointment in London was that of lecturer on anatomy at the Aldersgate Street School of Medicine in 1831. Two years later he became lecturer on anatomy at the Westminster Hospital Medical School, and it was while there that he projected his great work, the "Cyclopædia of Anatomy and Physiology."

The Council of King's College invited Bentley Todd, then aged twenty-seven, to occupy the Chair of Physio-

ROBERT BENTLEY TODD, F.R.S.
1809–1860

(*Bust dated* 1860 *by M. Noble* (1818–76) *in the possession of the Royal College of Surgeons of England*)

To face p. 110

logy in succession to Herbert Mayo, F.R.S., surgeon at the Middlesex Hospital, who had been appointed the first professor of anatomy, morbid anatomy and physiology in the newly constituted Medical Department of King's College, in July, 1830. This invitation Todd readily accepted, and commenced a memorable professorship on August 19th, 1836. In the same year he took an *ad eundem* M.D. degree through Pembroke College, Oxford.

Todd proved himself to be such a successful and delightful lecturer in physiology, a subject then almost in its infancy, that he drew a large number of students to his classes from other medical schools. In consequence of this some of the medical schools of the Metropolis soon followed the example of King's College and appointed their special lecturers in physiology.

Todd did his utmost to advance the physiological work in which he was engaged; his lectures and teaching excited the interest of his students, and he encouraged scientific investigations amongst his pupils in every way possible. Todd, however, did not neglect the cultivation of medicine; he became physician to the Western Dispensary and to the Royal Infirmary for Children. He soon found, however, that these two appointments did not provide him with sufficient clinical experience, and, moreover, supported by his colleagues in the Medical Department of King's College, he was soon able to persuade the Council of the College of the importance of founding a hospital in connection with the College in order that the students of the Medical Department might have the advantage of instruction in clinical work by their own College professors and teachers.

There is no doubt that it was mainly due to the untiring efforts and restless energy of Bentley Todd, supported as he was by William Cotton, T. G. Sambrooke and Robert Cheere, that King's College Hospital was founded in 1839.

He took an active part in the negotiations, which extended over many months, and acted as honorary secretary to the appeal fund. He was appointed physician to the new hospital in 1840. More than once Todd has been referred to as the distinguished founder of King's College Hospital. In the Physiological Department of the College Todd soon obtained the assistance of William Bowman.

Bowman joined the Medical Department of King's College in October, 1837. He, at the age of sixteen, had been apprenticed to Joseph H. Hodgson, F.R.S., surgeon to the Birmingham General Hospital, and there he spent five years of study. At the Birmingham Hospital Bowman came under the direct notice of Dr. Peyton Blakiston, one of the physicians at that institution. Blakiston obtained Bowman's co-operation in connection with his investigations on the structure of cardiac muscle, and in return he presented Bowman with a compound microscope.

There is no doubt that Todd was always foremost in his physiological researches, and he laid it down that no physiological conclusions ought to be drawn without an intimate acquaintance with the minute structure of the human body. At that period the microscope had recently come into use, and there is also no doubt that Bowman, with his previous medical training at Birmingham and his newly acquired microscope, was of the greatest help to Todd in his physiological and histological investigations. Todd, on the other hand, must have exercised a profound influence upon Bowman and inspired and directed him in his microscopical researches. In their work at King's College they eventually became intimately associated, and in 1848 Bowman was appointed joint professor of physiology with Todd.

The lectures were then divided: Todd dealt with digestion, respiration, circulation and the nervous system;

Bowman with the minute structure of the tissues, the organs of sense, secretion and reproduction. Together they edited the "Cyclopædia of Anatomy and Physiology," four volumes of which appeared between 1836 and 1859. In producing this work they obtained the collaboration of the leading scientific men of the period both at home and abroad. This cyclopædia did more to encourage and advance the study of physiology and comparative and microscopic anatomy than any book which had been previously published. Their joint work on the "Physiological Anatomy and Physiology of Man" became a standard text-book of that period, in which the authors reminded their readers that "a correct physiology must ever be the foundation of rational medicine." This work was published in two volumes. The first volume appeared in February, 1843; a second edition came out in 1856. The second volume, dedicated to Sir Benjamin Collins Brodie, Bart., was not published until 1859. In its production the authors had the valuable co-operation of Dr. Lionel Beale, then the sole occupant of the Chair of Physiology at King's College, and the assistance of Dr. H. Hyde Salter. This treatise formed the model upon which many subsequent works on anatomy and physiology published on the Continent were constructed.

Bentley Todd was a born organiser and endowed with boundless energy. At King's College he laboured vigorously and incessantly to advance the Medical Department which he had been instrumental in resuscitating. With the help of the three distinguished principals of the College, the Rev. Hugh James Rose, the Rev. John Lonsdale and the Rev. William Jelf, he set to work to emancipate the staff of the Medical Department from the somewhat excessive burden of the religious tests imposed by the Council of the College; to encourage medical education by the

9

introduction of scholarships; and to improve the discipline and the supervision of the work of the medical students by introducing the collegiate system, whereby rooms in the uppermost story of the College were set aside for the use of resident students. This provision of apartments in the College was made specially in the interest of the medical students, many of whom came to King's College from the provinces.

Todd taught that the religious and moral duties of a doctor are just as important as practical and scientific attainment, and, with the help of the Rev. Hugh J. Rose, did his utmost to instil religious principles into the students placed under his charge. Bentley Todd also advocated the appointment of one of the medical professors of the College as Dean of the Medical Department in order that the detailed arrangements of the department might be under the general direction of that official. It was, however, pointed out that as the office of Dean would be one of labour and of considerable responsibility, it ought to be held by the professors in turn. The first Dean to hold office was Todd himself, and, appointed in 1842, he did duty for one year. He was again elected to the office in 1845 which he resigned in 1846.

After occupying the Chair of Physiology at King's College for seventeen years, Todd, through pressure of private engagements, was obliged to resign (January, 1853). He delivered his farewell physiological address to the students at King's College on March 21st, 1853. During his professorship he had been the chief directing and almost irresistible force in the Medical Department of King's, and on receipt of his letter of resignation the Council of the College became greatly perturbed. A sub-committee of the Council was appointed to consider the situation which had arisen. His resignation at the College involved his resignation at the hospital, since the office of physician to the hospital was attached to a college professorship. So strong, however, was the desire on the part of the College Council and hospital medical staff to retain the services of Todd as a physician to the hospital that on February 25th, 1853, the rule which connected the two posts was rescinded, and Todd, though released from the College, retained his post as physician to the hospital. It was hoped that Bowman, who had been joint professor with Todd, would have been able to undertake the whole duties of the Chair of Physiology at King's College, but increasing demands upon his time in connection with the clinical side of his professional work prevented him from so doing, and consequently, in 1853, Lionel S. Beale was appointed joint professor of Physiology with Bowman.

At the hospital Todd, a physiological physician, was a great clinical teacher. When lecturing by the bedside his teaching was simple and clear; he seldom referred to notes. His instruction was eminently demonstrative and practical, and he charmed his students into an irresistible attention. He frequently made practical application of the truths he was endeavouring to enunciate, and in this manner his experience as a physician exercised a reflected influence on his teaching as a physiologist. He impressed upon his pupils the necessity of accurate and intelligent clinical observation and of right diagnosis before treatment should be adopted.

Amongst his clinical clerks at King's were Lionel Beale, David Conway Evans, William and James Hyde Salter.

Bentley Todd's three volumes of "Clinical Lectures" were outstanding. The first, published in 1856, was on "Paralysis, Certain Diseases of the Brain, and Other Affections of the Nervous System"; the second, "On Certain Diseases of the Urinary Organs, and on Dropsies," appeared in 1857; the third and last volume, "On Certain Acute Diseases," completed only a month before his death, was published in 1860.

Todd held strong views on the treatment of acute diseases, and these were embodied in the last volume of his clinical lectures, which he dedicated "To the Former and Present House Physicians and Clinical Clerks of King's College Hospital." He had for a long time laboured not only to teach but to apply in practice his belief that antiphlogistic treatment was unnecessary for the cure of certain acute diseases, *i.e.*, inflammation and fever. Such conditions had been previously treated by bleeding and the use of calomel, antimony and lowering remedies generally.

Todd's views are embodied in the following propositions:

(1) That the notion, so long prevalent in the schools, that acute disease can be prevented or cured by means which depress and reduce vital and nervous power is altogether fallacious.

(2) That acute disease is not curable by the direct influence of any form of drug or any known remedial agent, except when it is capable of acting as an antidote or of neutralising a poison on the presence of which in the system the disease may depend.

(3) That the disease is cured by natural processes, to promote which, in their full vigour, vital power must be upheld. Remedies, whether in the shape of drugs which exercise a special physiological influence on the system, or in whatever form, are useful only so far as they may excite, assist or promote these natural curative processes.

(4) That it should be the aim of the physician (after he has sedulously studied the clinical history of the disease and made himself master of its diagnosis) to inquire minutely into the ultimate nature of these curative processes—their

physiology, so to speak—to discover the best means of assisting them, to search for antidotes to morbid poisons, and to ascertain the best and most convenient means of upholding vital power.

He also wrote: "Alcohol, in some form or other, is a remedy whose value can scarcely, I think, be over-estimated, and one upon which, when carefully administered, I rely with the utmost confidence in a great number of cases of disease which are at all amenable to treatment. Alcohol may be employed in all those diseases in which a tendency to depression of the vital powers exists, and there are no acute diseases in which this lowering tendency is not present." Todd taught that the vital powers of the patient should be upheld by the administration of brandy, which he prescribed in "low diseases" in doses as much as one or even two ounces every hour over a short period.

Although his clinical lectures were full of most valuable practical illustrations, his therapeutics did not meet with general approval and were not generally accepted. It is, however, only fair to state that mild cases of fever and inflammation were treated by him without stimulants, or at any rate in but moderate quantities.

The supporting plan of treatment in cases of fever had, however, been advocated in 1833 by Dr. R. J. Graves, who, like Todd, had been a teacher of physiology, and similar supporting treatment had been carried out by Dr. Peyton Blakiston during an epidemic of influenza in Birmingham in 1837.

In referring to Todd's "Clinical Lectures," a reviewer wrote: "For lessons in clinical pathology we know not any volumes to which the student may be referred with more advantage than the series of Dr. Todd's 'Clinical Lectures.'" These fifty lectures were re-edited and published in one volume by Todd's pupil, Lionel Beale, in 1861.

In 1843 Todd published a treatise " On Gout, Rheumatic Fever and Chronic Rheumatism of the Joints." He also contributed a memoir upon the " Anatomy of the Brain, Spinal Cord and Ganglions " (1845) ; " The Physiology of the Nervous System " in 1847, and in the same year " On the Contractility and Irritability of the Muscles of Paralysed Limbs and their Excitability to the Galvanic Current in Comparison with the Corresponding Muscles of Healthy Limbs."

The late James Collier, in his Harveian Oration, delivered before the Royal College of Physicians of London on October 8th, 1934, referred to Todd's remarkable clinical insight in nervous diseases, and he referred particularly to peripheral neuritis and locomotor ataxy.

Peripheral Neuritis.—Todd, in an attempt to explain lead paralysis to his pupils, said : " I believe that the muscles and nerves are early affected and that at a later period the nerve centres may become implicated. The nervous system is thus first affected at its periphery in the muscles and nerves, and, the poisonous influence continuing, the contamination gradually advances towards the centre." Collier wrote : " Recently it has been shown by Aub and others that in lead paralysis accumulation of the lead occurs first in the affected muscles, and that the poison seeps up through the nerve endings into the nerves and reaches the central nervous system."

Tabes Dorsalis.—" Todd was the first to begin the breaking up of the spinal diseases, at that time all classed as 'paraplegia,' by his remarkable invention of locomotor ataxy as a distinct clinical entity. He did this with his usual vivid imagination and his customary absolute faith in his own powers of clinical and post-mortem observation."

When about twenty-four years of age Todd wrote on " Paralysis " in Forbes, Tweedie and Conolly's Dictionary, published in 1834, in which he corrected Bell's functions of the facial nerve ; he also described the sensory element in sphincter control and explained how its loss accounted for retention. He formulated the term "astereognostic loss," and he described spinal hemiplegia, cerebral paraplegia due to bilateral lesions, and Brown-Sequard's paralysis from local injury. Collier further wrote that "Todd was by far the greatest clinical neurologist Britain had produced until the time of Hughlings Jackson" (*b.* 1835).

There is no doubt that Bentley Todd with Robert James Graves (1796–1853) and A. Trousseau were the most eminent and illustrious clinical teachers of the last century. Todd worked hard to change the whole practice of medicine, to root out the blind acceptance of what was at that period routine practice, and to point out the necessity of accurate diagnosis before treatment should be adopted.

At the Royal College of Physicians of London Todd was Censor in 1839–40, in 1847–8, and in 1852. In 1839 he was Goulstonian Lecturer, his subject being "The Physiology of the Stomach" ; Croonian Lecturer in 1843, when he made "Practical Remarks on Gout, Rheumatic Fever and Chronic Rheumatism of Joints" ; Lumleian Lecturer in 1849, when he discussed the "Pathology and Treatment of Convulsive Diseases," and showed that many cases of delirium and coma were to be explained upon the supposition of blood poisoning, and did not depend upon any lesion of the central nervous system.

It was largely through the influence of Bentley Todd, together with his colleague William Bowman, his pupil Lionel Beale, and with the co-operation of the Bishop of London, that St. John's House and Sisterhood, Queen's Square, Westminster, was founded in 1848 as a training institution on a religious basis for nurses. In great measure through Todd's influence, on March 31st, 1856, an agreement was reached between the Committee of Management of King's College Hospital and the Committee of St. John's House whereby the nursing at King's was to be placed under the direction of that institution ; and in May, 1856, the Lady Superior of St. John's House, with a staff of nurses, entered upon their duties at King's College Hospital. This arrangement continued until 1885.

In July and August, 1859, Todd was called to give evidence for the prosecution in a remarkable case in which a Doctor Thomas Smethurst was eventually convicted of poisoning his mistress, Isabella Banks, whom he had bigamously married. Ten medical men for the prosecution, of whom Todd was one, gave evidence to the effect that she was poisoned, and seven who appeared for the defence said that, in their opinion, she died from natural causes, either from dysentery, or from dysentery and the effects of pregnancy. There was much controversy and a great outcry, especially in the medical world, against the conviction. Subsequently Smethurst was granted a reprieve, and received a free pardon.

In a long letter to *The Times*, written from Vevey, Switzerland, on September 5th, 1859, Todd appears to have summed up the case, and stated that in his opinion Isabella Banks died from the effects of frequent doses of antimony and bichloride of mercury, with occasional doses of arsenic. He concluded by writing : "I trust this very important case will not be lost upon toxicologists, and that it will lead to new and careful observations upon the effects of poisons in combination, upon their mode of elimination, upon the means which may be used to prevent the accumulation of them in the tissues and organs of the body, and, finally, that it will induce analytical chemists to review carefully all the processes hitherto in use for the purpose of detecting mineral and other poisons with a view to clear up every possible source of fallacy."

In December, 1859, through increasing private practice, Todd felt compelled to resign his active work at King's College Hospital; he was at once appointed consulting physician. In his farewell lecture to the students at King's, delivered only six weeks before his death, he inculcated, in his usual clear and decided manner, his views on the great value of clinical teaching, in which he was so great an adept.

At the end of January, 1860, he was summoned to Wales to attend a patient; he returned to Shrewsbury on Sunday, January 29th, and during the night vomiting set in, which was followed by an attack of hæmatemesis. With his characteristic energy Todd took the early train to London on Monday morning, and although feeling far from well saw his patients at his house. At midday Dr. Edward Liveing happened to call upon him and found him very ill. Early in the afternoon a fresh attack of hæmatemesis occurred, and Dr. Thomas Watson, Dr. Latham, Dr. Armitage and Mr. William Bowman were sent for. In spite of treatment, hæmorrhage continued and he died at 8 p.m. on Monday, January 30th. A post-mortem examination was made by Dr. Lionel Beale and Mr. John Wood; they discovered advanced cirrhosis of the liver with extensive hæmorrhage into the stomach, duodenum and ileum, and the kidneys were enlarged.

To the medical profession Todd's death was a great loss. He was one of the most popular physicians of his day and his opinion on an obscure or doubtful case was of the greatest possible service. It was felt that the public generally had lost a physician whose kindness was in no way inferior to his skill; and his friends deplored the death of one who was a real friend and who spared no pains or trouble in helping those who required his aid. He was buried at Kensal Green Cemetery on Saturday, February 4th, 1860, in the presence of over two hundred medical men, many of whom had been his former students.

Lionel Beale wrote of Todd : " Measured by time, his life was short, but his labours were great. Few men in the same number of years have done more. When he came to King's College there were but few pupils in the Medical Department and no hospital. He lived to see the medical school of King's become one of the best in the country and remarkable as the nursery of many medical teachers and scientific investigators."

The Todd Memorial Fund.—It was generally felt that the existence of King's College Hospital was due in the first place to the foresight and the exertions of Bentley Todd, and it was the regret of those who knew him and admired his work that he did not live to see the second hospital building completed in 1861.

A public meeting was held on February 15th, 1860, to consider the question of a fitting memorial to Todd, and a sub-committee was appointed to consider the details of such a memorial. It was finally agreed to place a statue of Todd in the main hall of the new King's College Hospital (1861), and to found an annual prize at King's College to perpetuate his memory as an accomplished physiologist and an illustrious teacher of clinical medicine. The statue, by Noble, is now in the centre of the courtyard of King's College Hospital, and faces Denmark Hill. The Todd Prize for clinical medicine consists of a bronze medal and books worth four guineas, and is awarded annually. Recently the value of the prize has been increased. The Todd ward in King's College Hospital is named after its illustrious founder.

Reference has been made to *King's College Hospital*

Reports, volume iv; "The Centenary History of King's College," by F. J. C. Hearnshaw, M.A., LL.D.; "The Trial of Dr. Thomas Smethurst," by Leonard A. Parry, M.D., B.S., F.R.C.S.; *The Lancet*, 1860; *British Medical Journal*, 1870; "King's and Some King's Men," by H. Willoughby Lyle, M.D., F.R.C.S. London, 1935.

H. W. L.

XV JAMES YOUNG SIMPSON
(1811–1870)

MIDWIFE AND INTRODUCER OF CHLOROFORM

A DIFFERENT type of personality from that depicted for Lord Lister [p. 137] is presented by Sir James Y. Simpson. Both of these men made outstanding contributions to medicine which have been among the greatest boons to humanity, both stood high in popular estimation during their lifetime, and both were men of deep religious conviction, but there the comparison ends. While Lister enjoyed from the outset all the advantages of financial prosperity and of early scientific training, Simpson affords an example, not uncommon under the democratic educational conditions in Scotland, of a youth rising from a family of slight means to high professional and social position.

James Y. Simpson was the seventh son of David Simpson, a baker with a small business at Bathgate, in Linlithgowshire, and was born on June 7th, 1811. His ancestors for many generations had been farmers in the district. This class in earlier days of the Scottish Lowlands was noted for its habits of diligence and self-reliance, formed by laborious work in youth. These habits had often secured for their possessors high standing in the church, at the bar, in medicine, in commerce or in foreign service.

The boy was sent to the village school at the age of four, and was early noted for his quick apprehension, love of books, and retentive memory. Lessons came easily to him, and he was generally dux of his class, although he also

JAMES YOUNG SIMPSON
1811–1870
(*From the portrait by Macbeth, in possession of the University of Edinburgh*)

To face p. 124

entered heartily into boyish sports. The district of Linlithgow is one full of antiquarian associations, and Simpson from his boyhood developed a taste for enquiry into these, which in later life bore fruit in his numerous archæological papers. There existed in Scotland of the eighteenth and nineteenth centuries, among the social class to which the Simpsons belonged, a widespread ambition that one at least of the family should be educated for a learned profession. Accordingly at the age of fourteen, with the support of his elder brothers, Simpson entered Edinburgh University, where for three years he attended classes in Latin, Greek, mathematics and philosophy.

In 1827 he enrolled as a medical student, one of his favourite teachers being Robert Liston, who came from near Bathgate, and who was still an extra-academical lecturer on surgery at Edinburgh. Simpson's notebooks show the unusual feature of free critical remarks upon the opinions that his teachers expressed. This questioning habit, unusual in a student, which in maturer years was strongly marked, may have been learned from Liston, who never hesitated to express adverse opinions of his contemporaries. On one occasion, after seeing the agony of a poor Highland woman under amputation of the breast, Simpson decided to give up medicine, and started to seek work as a writer's clerk, but on second thoughts he returned to his medical studies, determining that if possible he would discover something to make operations less painful. Before the age of nineteen he obtained the licence of the Royal College of Surgeons, Edinburgh, and became assistant to Dr. Gairdner, a well-known Edinburgh practitioner, and in 1832 he received the M.D. degree with a thesis on "Death from Inflammation." After graduation, Simpson became for some years assistant to Dr. John Thomson, professor of pathology, with a salary of £50 a year, and this sufficed for all his wants. On Thomson's advice, which agreed with his own wishes, he resolved to devote himself to the study of obstetric medicine. He had already, during the two years of waiting till he should be old enough to receive the M.D. degree, attended practical courses of midwifery under Professor Hamilton and Dr. Thatcher.

An early paper, pathological and obstetrical, on diseases of the placenta, attracted great attention, and was reproduced in German, French and Italian medical journals. A visit to the medical schools of England and France was undertaken in 1835 with the financial help of his brothers, and in company with Dr. Douglas Maclagan, who was later professor of medical jurisprudence at Edinburgh. The notes made by Simpson on this tour show the same avidity for information and interrogation that he had displayed in his student days. His name was now becoming widely known, and in 1836 he was elected a corresponding member of the Medical Society of Ghent, the first of a long list of foreign honours conferred upon him. In this year he was appointed house surgeon to the Lying-in Hospital, under Professor Hamilton, and two years later he took over the extra-academical class of lectures on obstetric medicine from Dr. Mackintosh. He became immediately so successful as a lecturer that the members of his class at the end of the first session presented him with an address expressing their appreciation of his efforts. His extraordinary capacity for work is shown by correspondence at this time, in which he mentioned that after going late to bed, he was up at three in the morning busy in the preparation of lectures and papers. He now moved out of lodgings and took a house at 1 Dean Terrace, Edinburgh, where, as he wrote to a friend, he was engrossed all the time with "plenishing, patients and papers," but, nevertheless, he was again obliged to have recourse to his brothers for financial help.

In 1839 Professor Hamilton resigned the midwifery chair at Edinburgh University, and Simpson, although only twenty-eight years of age, announced himself as a candidate. He had become engaged to Miss Jessie Grindlay, of Liverpool, and the marriage was hurried on, so as to remove what was urged against him as a disqualification for the chair—the fact of his being unmarried. A professorial appointment in those days provoked as much general excitement as a Parliamentary election does now, and the canvass for the chair proceeded with great vigour, Simpson's testimonials extending to 200 printed pages. The candidates for the post were numerous, the most formidable being Dr. Kennedy, of Dublin, but on the day of election the thirty-three members of Town Council, who were the electors, voted seventeen for Dr. Simpson, and sixteen for Dr. Kennedy.

Simpson now threw himself with unabated vigour into the work of the chair, with the added practice and the desirability of more research which his position brought. He removed to 22 Albany Street for several years, until he took the house at 52 Queen Street, which has become specially associated with his name.

In spite of the great amount of work which his large class and rapidly increasing obstetric practice involved, he found time to gratify his love of antiquarian research by preparing his monumental work on the leper houses of Britain, involving nearly 500 references to old charters, registers of monasteries, records of town councils, old Acts of Parliament, English, Scottish and French histories, etc., which appeared in 1841. His papers on literary and antiquarian subjects, all involving much research and often affording strikingly original suggestions, were continued from time to time for the remainder of his life. These included subjects such as " Was the Roman Army Provided with Medical Officers ? " ; " Syphilis in Scotland in the 15th and 16th Centuries " ; " The Tombstone of the Grandfather of Hengist and Horsa " ; and " Cup Markings in Scotland, England and other Countries."

Simpson did not produce any single large work, but he was constantly busy in writing addresses to societies, descriptions of new instruments and methods, and controversial pamphlets concerned with medical organisation, teaching and conduct, usually short but masterly and exhaustive, and supporting the view he wished to enforce by erudite and recondite lore.

Articles of originality and of the highest quality dealing with the pathology and practical improvement of obstetric medicine flowed in rapid succession from his pen, including " The Pathology and Treatment of Uterine Diseases " ; " Clinical Lectures on Midwifery " ; " The Treatment of Unavoidable Hæmorrhage " ; " Ovariotomy " ; " Post-partum Hæmorrhage " ; " Removal of Cervical Carcinoma " ; " The Influence of Galvanism During Labour " ; etc. The new obstetric forceps and the uterine sound, which he devised, were marked by the simplicity of genius, and added greatly to the possibilities of assistance in delivery and of gynæcological treatment. He may be said to have practically created gynæcology as a scientific branch of medicine.

Simpson's name is prominently associated with anæsthesia, and the part that he played in its introduction was a great one. The early history of this subject is buried in antiquity, but towards the end of 1846, Morton, in America, had made public his success with the administration of ether by inhalation in surgical operations, and Liston, at University College Hospital, at once adopted it in surgery. Simpson, who had long been desiring to find some means to relieve the pains of childbirth, eagerly seized upon this new method, and, writing to a friend, remarked: "It is a glorious thought, I can think of naught else." Ether, administered as it then was by the open method, often proved unsuccessful, and Simpson, while using it in midwifery, set about investigating the anæsthetic properties of a large number of volatile substances, including chloride of hydrocarbon, nitrate of ethyl, benzene, bisulphide of carbon, etc. These he tried upon the persons of himself and his assistants, but discarded them for various reasons, until on November 15th, 1847, he found that chloroform, which had been recently discovered, and which had been suggested to him by Mr. Waldie, of Liverpool, as a likely substance for his purpose, fulfilled all his requirements.

Simpson, however, deserves credit for much more than the introduction of chloroform. Strange as it may seem at the present day, there was an immense amount of ignorance, superstition, objection on religious grounds, and scientific jealousy to be overcome before the use of anæsthesia was established, and Simpson had to exert great efforts by speeches, writings and practice in order to popularise anæsthesia with the profession and with the public. Only a man of his outstanding position and fame could have done this.

Less happy than anæsthesia was his introduction of acupressure in 1864, as a means of avoiding septic ligatures in the control of hæmorrhage, a matter which provoked the animosity of some of his surgical colleagues, who regarded it as an invasion of their province.

Far above Simpson's reputation as a writer and his credit for the introduction of anæsthesia was his celebrity in his own lifetime, as an outcome of his impressive personality. His temper was imperturbable. He was forbearing and forgiving at a time when animosities were bitter. He was kindly in manner and in act. He was a tireless worker, and, above all, he possessed what has been described as a magnetic attraction. People came to see him from every part of the world. The hotels and lodging houses of Edinburgh were crowded with his patients. Since the time of the great Dutch physician, of whom it is said that a letter from China addressed simply "Dr. Boerhaave, Europe," was duly delivered, probably no medical man has been so widely known as Simpson. Sir Robert Christison, in his "Autobiography," gives a vivid picture of Simpson's practice as he saw it on the occasion of a call at 52 Queen Street: "Simpson was at this period in the full swing of his marvellous practice. When I called for him his two reception rooms were, as usual, full of patients, more were seated in the lobby, female faces stared from all the windows in vacant expectancy, and a lady was ringing the door-bell. But the doctor brushed through the crowd to join me, and left them all kicking their heels at their leisure for the next two hours." In 1866 Her Majesty Queen Victoria offered him a baronetcy.

Simpson died, virtually worn out by his labours, at the age of fifty-nine, on May 6th, 1870. He had had several attacks of angina pectoris, and after death an aneurysm of the heart was discovered. His resting-place is in Warriston Cemetery, Edinburgh, and his popularity was attested by the dense crowd which attended his funeral, collected from the whole city and neighbouring country.

J. D. C.

SIR JAMES PAGET, F.R.S.
1814–1899

(From the portrait, painted in 1871 by Sir J. E. Millais, in the Great Hall of St. Bartholomew's Hospital)

To face p. 131

XVI JAMES PAGET
(1814–1899)

CONSULTING SURGEON

It was said by the wise man of old : " Count no man happy until he be dead." The tale of Sir James Paget's life has long been completed, and he can fairly be said to have been amongst the fortunate few who enjoyed real happiness. Without any advantage of rank or fortune he rose to be the most trusted and well-beloved surgeon in the long reign of Queen Victoria. For two generations he knew us. My father was one of his pupils when Paget was still Warden of the College at St. Bartholomew's Hospital, and from him received an invitation to apply for the post of Professor of Anatomy at Edinburgh, when John Goodsir resigned and his place was long and worthily filled by Sir William Turner. My elementary education was carried out at the school in Regent's Park, which was founded by Paget's father-in-law, who also sent his sons there. Later in life, when I was a young graduate fresh from Oxford and he was at the height of his success, he would invite me to breakfast—the only spare time in his busy day—to discuss those manuscripts which afterwards appeared as a history of English surgery, with his well-written and well-considered introduction. I then learnt some of the secrets of his success : a perfect home life, a gracious wife who saved him trouble in every possible way, an unruffled temper, and so strict an economist of time that he was always punctual, and was never hurried. There were other factors, too, which contributed in no small degree to his eminence. A complete simplicity of character, and no attempt at show. He was living in a small house in Harewood Place, which was shut off from Oxford Street by a locked gate, preventing the short street from becoming a thoroughfare. There was a tiny garden within the area railings of the house, and there were two rooms on the ground floor, the one used as a dining room and after breakfast as the waiting room, the other a study and consulting room. Through these two rooms passed all that was remarkable or difficult in surgery and personages whose names have become historical. Rich and poor alike were treated with the same courtesy and care. Those who could afford it paid a guinea for the consultation. Paget was no seeker after money, and there were some who said that as his name became famous he should have charged more, but that was not his way. He was practising a profession, not a trade, and, as always, he was setting an example to his pupils. His religious principles were never obtruded, but they were deeply implanted. So long as he was Warden of the College at St. Bartholomew's Hospital he never missed the early morning service in the little Church of St. Bartholomew-the-Less within the gates of the hospital. Later in life most Sunday mornings saw him walking down Oxford Street on his way to St. Paul's Cathedral. His deep religious feelings he transmitted to his children. Two of his sons were consecrated Bishops, the one of Oxford, the other of Chester, and the beautiful writings of his youngest son, Stephen, breathe the same spirit.

To the world at large Paget was known as one of the first English surgical pathologists. He used the microscope at a time when there were no laboratories, and a naked-eye examination was alone usual; he followed the teaching of Johannes Müller, of Schleiden and of Schwann, and he did much to put the classification and structure of tumours upon a satisfactory footing. As a young man he made his name by cataloguing the Anatomical and Pathological Museum at St. Bartholomew's Hospital. He described the specimens in good English, and as far as possible appended a note of the clinical history. The love of morbid anatomy never left him, and long afterwards he did good service for the Museum of the Royal College of Surgeons at Lincoln's Inn Fields His example fired a younger generation, and a school of surgical pathologists rose—men like Goodhart, Target, Alban Doran, Shattock and Beadles—who all looked to Paget as their master. They in turn trained their successors to the lasting benefit of collections of morbid anatomy throughout the country. It thus happened that Paget became better known for his wise advice and his skill in diagnosis than for his operative excellence. As his son said in the " Memoirs and Letters of Sir James Paget " : " It was roughly expressed in a saying that was current at the time : 'You ought to go to Paget to find out what is the matter with you, and then go to Fergusson to have it removed.' " His highest excellence was not in operating, but in his calculation of all the complex forces at work on a patient—heredity, temperament, habits, previous illnesses ; in his insight into the variations and abnormalities of disease ; in his pathological knowledge of the characters, tendencies and developments of surgical diseases ; and in all these he was easily the superior of his contemporaries.

Paget went from honour to honour throughout his life. Elected assistant surgeon to St. Bartholomew's Hospital in 1847 in the face of great opposition, his character had already marked him out the first Warden of the College for the students founded in 1843. In due course he became surgeon and lecturer, first on physiology, afterwards on surgery in the medical school. He was Serjeant-Surgeon to Queen

Victoria, and was President of the Royal College of Surgeons in 1875. As early as 1851 he was elected a Fellow of the Royal Society. Among the thirty-eight candidates the council selected fifteen, and "I was the only candidate for whom the whole council voted. Nothing of the kind could be more gratifying," he added, writing to one of his brothers, "it comes of being peaceable." In 1871 the honour of a baronetcy was conferred upon him.

All his talents were brought into use when he acted as President of the International Congress which was held in London in 1881, and it was a brilliant success under his skilful guidance. His introductory address was a wonderful performance, carefully thought out and delivered in the flawless language of which he was a master. Eleven years later he left Harewood Place, and moved to 5 Park Square West, Regent's Park. Here Lady Paget, his beloved wife, died in 1895, and he himself followed her peacefully on Saturday, December 30th, 1899. The first part of the funeral service was in Westminster Abbey, and he was buried by the side of his wife in the cemetery at Finchley.

It is not difficult now to place Paget in his right place in relation to Victorian Surgery. His greatest achievement, perhaps, was that he raised the surgeon in public estimation and caused surgery to hold its present high position in the social scale. A few surgeons before him had been gentlemen: Richard Wiseman, Charles Barnard and Benjamin Brodie were gentlemen, but the standard of gentility in the Caroline and Georgian periods differed greatly from our own. Then followed a period when surgeons returned to their rough and uncouth ways. They were not ashamed to hold the attention of their pupils in lecture by the telling of nasty stories, and they quarrelled bitterly amongst themselves. Paget brought peace, gentleness, pureness of mind, absolute honesty in thought and deed, courtesy to all, perfect facility in speaking and a very pleasant voice. As a surgeon he was fortunate in his time. The introduction of anæsthetics reduced the horrors and anxiety of the operating theatre. Anxiety so great that it sent some like John Flint South of St. Thomas's to seek aid in prayer before he operated; others like Abernethy to vomit, and even so hardened an operator as Astley Cooper to feel that "much had been taken out of him." Paget, too, escaped the drudgery of teaching anatomy, usually the lot of the younger aspirants for surgery. Paget graduated through the school of morbid anatomy. He never had to associate with resurrectionists: it was his business to dissect and describe museum preparations in comparative comfort. Yet as a surgeon he was not greatly in advance of his time. His knowledge of German and his use of the microscope enabled him to improve morbid anatomy, whilst his literary skill gave his lectures on Pathology a very wide circle of readers. It was, however, all personal knowledge derived from books and his own observation. Until late in life he never left England and had no first-hand acquaintance with foreign laboratories and methods of working. Nor was this surprising, foreign travel was difficult and expensive when he was young and had neither money nor patients, whilst his inability to speak French or German fluently would in any case have made matters hard for him. He had, too, a strong herd instinct and preferred to take his whole family with him when he travelled. Besides, the English hospital surgeons of his generation rarely went far afield. They took a holiday regularly for a month or six weeks in the summer to allow the assistant surgeon a little time to get practical experience in operating, but rarely went farther than to a house in the home counties where they chafed to get back to their hospital duties.

Great changes took place in the practice of an operating surgeon during Paget's lifetime. Improved surgical teaching and the establishment of local centres in the Provinces lessened the supremacy of London. This led to the abolition of itinerant surgeons, that is to say, of surgeons who were called long distances to operate and advise. Railways enabled the patient to come to the surgeon instead of the surgeon going to the patient, and thus arose a class of consultants of whom Paget was one of the earliest and certainly one of the most outstanding.

D'A. P.

[*Elliott & Fry*

LORD LISTER, O.M., F.R.S.
1827–1912

To face p. 137

XVII JOSEPH LISTER
(1827–1912)

THE FOUNDER OF MODERN SURGERY

DISRAELI tells us that " one of the greatest legacies of any nation is the memory of a great man, and the inheritance of a great example." Such an outstanding example was Joseph Lister.

Any student of history knows how difficult it is to determine the true author of any movement, the chief leader of any great adventure, the first discoverer of any fresh truth, or any new country. America had been " discovered " by other explorers before Columbus. Many mariners had doubtless been wrecked on its coasts ; others, who returned safely to Europe, had not the enterprise and courage to make good their discovery. So, before the days of Lister, antiseptics had been used—including carbolic acid —and the " germ theory of suppuration " had been anticipated before Pasteur. But by universal acceptance, Lister's name will always stand out as the creator of modern surgery, just as Harvey's does as the discoverer of the circulation of the blood, and Jenner's as the founder of vaccine therapy.

Many things combined to make Lister the greatest master of surgery—the times, the occasions, and the man himself. The last was the prime factor. The world, as in so many movements, was awaiting both the hour and the man. It was the heroic mould in which Lister was cast that brought to fruition the sowing of centuries. Without his great soul the harvest might still be delayed, and we would not now be living in the golden age of medicine and surgery. In the case of many labourers in the field of science, the personal character of the worker may be looked on as of negligible or secondary importance. In the creation of antiseptic surgery it was not so. Those whose great privilege it was to work with him are, in spite of their very various characters, unanimous in what might be called their " hero-worship," and also in their recognition that it was his noble character which made him the heir of all the medical ages.

The lives of scientific men are usually passed in the cool, sequestered vale of life, so that few of them present the picturesque happenings which give a more histrionic interest to the careers of statesmen, politicians, sailors, soldiers, explorers or adventurers ; yet Lister's life had much in it of colour and change, with the zest which a long and gallant—and victorious—struggle always arouses.

Joseph Lister was a " true-born Englishman." None of the nations which make up our United Kingdom can claim that he had any " Celtic fringe." His people came from Yorkshire, and his father was a prosperous wine merchant in the City of London. This prosperity was an undoubted factor in the making of the future master of medicine. He never felt the carking care of pence, for the competency supplied by his business parent allowed of his devoting himself whole-heartedly to the study of his profession and to the academic career, without any anxiety as to the business side of practice. From his father he inherited an equally valuable asset in a love of learning and science. For the wine merchant was deeply interested in the science of optics ; he helped to perfect the microscope, and was a Fellow of the Royal Society. Lister, from his family, also inherited the simple faith of the Quaker confraternity, and although he lived most of his life and died a member of the Church of England, the strict tenets in which his youth was passed explain how prepared he was to prefer peace to strife, and to shun delights and live laborious days.

He was born on April 5th, 1827, in the Queen Anne house known as Upton Lodge, in Essex, in what is now the Borough of West Ham. The house still exists untouched (it is the Vicarage of St. Peter's Parish), somewhat shorn of its grounds and orchards, an oasis buried in the mean streets which now connect it, by thundering trams and murdering motors, to the macrocosm of London. But a hundred years ago it was ten miles from the congested East End, and lay amidst the fields and woods where Lister learned that love of botany and bird life which gave him so much interest and happiness throughout his long life.

After attending private schools in Hitchin and Tottenham he, at the age of seventeen, and in the year 1844, entered University College, which appealed to him as a Quaker, for it had recently been founded as a non-sectarian institution. King's College had also been started, about the same time, to maintain the tenets of the Church of England. It is interesting to note that Lister began his academic career in one college and finished it in the other ; he is gratefully remembered in both Colleges and in the University of London, where he took his B.A. and his M.B. He also passed his F.R.C.S., and won all the scholarships and medals he met with on his way.

From London, at the age of twenty-six, he was attracted by the fame of Syme to Edinburgh, and there he had two strokes of good fortune—he became Syme's house-surgeon and married his daughter. From Edinburgh, at the early age of thirty-three, he was called to fill the Chair of Surgery in the University of Glasgow (1860). There he remained, evolving his principles and early practice of antiseptic surgery, until 1869. Then, at the age of forty-two, he returned to Edinburgh as Professor of Surgery, and there he passed the eight years of his life which he afterwards referred to as the happiest, as they certainly were the fullest and most flowing.

In 1877 Lister left Edinburgh for King's College Hospital, London, where he worked until the year 1893, when he retired at the age of sixty-six.

He was President of the Royal Society from 1895 to 1900. In 1903, for the first time, his stalwart frame was shaken by a threatening of the infirmities of age. His last years were saddened by slowly failing health, and on February 10th, 1912, in his eighty-fifth year, he died peacefully at the little town of Walmer, looking out on the English Channel. He had been made a baronet in 1883. In 1897, the year of Queen Victoria's second jubilee, he was created a peer on New Year's Day, his peerage being the first ever conferred on a surgeon.

Lister was given a public funeral in Westminster Abbey, and there is a marble medallion of his bust in the North transept, placed near to those of the great scientists, Darwin, Stokes, Adams and Watt. But, by his own directions, he was buried in West Hampstead Cemetery beside his devoted wife, who had died in 1893. They had no children.

It is, unfortunately, impossible in a short space to describe how Lister evolved the treatment of wounds. The slow, laborious, anxious, disappointing steps by which the technique of surgical dressings was changed from the complicated, contradictory and chaotic customs of centuries to the beautiful simplicity and security of to-day, would require more than a chapter to themselves. Carping critics were always content to attempt to belittle the great master's work, and a few even still strive to disparage it by suggesting that "aseptic" surgery is a better and even a different surgery to that known as "antiseptic." Unfortunately, mankind does not live by bread alone, but largely by catchwords. Lister appreciated the value of technique ; but in making, in decades, more progress than had been made in centuries, he refused to be tied down to one ritual. Besides, his constant anxiety was not to convert a stubborn world to the use of this, that, or the other method of dressing wounds, but to convince the profession of the soundness of his principles. These having been universally accepted, " most can raise the flower now, for all have got the seed." If mankind must have a label to distinguish modern surgical treatment from that of all preceding ages, there is only one word for it : surgery is now Listerian.

What was it like before the coming of Lister ? The results of surgical operation in the middle of last century were no better than in the days of Hippocrates. I think they may even have become worse since December 21st, 1846. On that day the first operation ever performed in this country under general anæsthesia (ether) was carried out in University College Hospital by Robert Liston. Lister, who happened to be house-surgeon at the time to Sir John Erichsen, was present at it. The introduction of general anæsthesia encouraged surgeons to attempt operations which formerly had not been possible. Wards which had previously been largely occupied by cases of fractures, dislocation and other non-operative cases, became crowded with suppurating, septic, surgical wounds, accompanied by the horrors which the present generation can with difficulty imagine.

Even with the extension of the field of surgery permitted by anæsthesia, the practice of surgery was still restricted largely to urgent conditions. While I was Lister's house-surgeon I never once saw him open an abdomen. I had helped him, greatly daring, to open a knee-joint in order to wire a fractured patella, and had heard him denounced at the Medical Society of London as deserving of a charge of manslaughter should one of his patients ever die as a result of " the unjustifiable risk entailed in opening a healthy joint." This shows that until Lister had demonstrated how to save life and limb in cases of compound fracture, and how joints could be opened with impunity, no progress had been made for at least three hundred years. For when Ambroise Paré (1517–90) was asked if the wound of the King of Navarre was mortal, he said : " Yes, because all wounds of great joints, and especially contused wounds, are mortal, according to all those who have written about them."

So little did Erichsen foresee the wondrous miracle to be wrought by his own house-surgeon that he committed himself, in 1874, to the prophecy that : " The abdomen, the chest and the brain would be for ever shut from the intrusion of the wise and humane surgeon." Another surgeon had pronounced that " an abdominal operation should be classed amongst the methods of the executioner."

Denonvilliers (1808–72), a surgeon to the Charité Hospital in Paris, used to say to his pupils last century : "When an operation is necessary think ten times about it, for too often when we decide upon an operation we sign the death warrant of the patient."

So limited was the practice of operative surgery in the middle of last century that Cockburn, writing in 1847, said : " The whole paying surgical practice of Scotland would scarcely keep one gentleman-like scalpel going." Yet these operative cases were sufficient to make all surgical wards of all the hospitals of the world reek with the stench of putrefaction.

The " hospital smell," often referred to even in the non-medical literature of those days, was looked upon as the inevitable accompaniment of a surgical ward. I remember the tin trays placed beneath an amputated stump put to catch the pus dripping from the gaping and festering flaps, from which hung the hemp ligatures left to secure the main arteries. In the post-mortem room we could see the "amyloid degeneration" which indicated the patient's long and weary passage to the grave, slowly consumed by hectic surgical fever. Others had reached the dead-house more speedily by such dread scourges as erysipelas, hospital gangrene, septicæmia and pyæmia.

My neighbour and friend, Sir Buckston Browne, writes to tell me that when he was house-surgeon to Erichsen in 1873, in the old University College Hospital, and in the very rooms where Lister had preceded him, his wards were almost decimated by "hospital gangrene"; and yet Sir Buckston's own son-in-law, Mr. Hugh Lett of the London Hospital, has never seen a single case! Such are the changes in our own lifetime.

The operative death-rate before the coming of Lister was from 25 to 40 per cent.; in other words, the chances were that one out of every three or four patients would die. In his own hands, in Lister's early years, the death-rate from amputation was 45 per cent. Sometimes, in military hospitals, the proportion would mount up to 75–90 per cent. At one time in the Krankenhaus of Munich, "80 per cent. of the wounds became affected with gangrene, and filled the surgical wards with horror." In the American Civil War almost all abdominal and head wounds proved fatal, and when the driver of an ambulance waggon was asked if he knew how to treat wounded men, he replied: "Oh yes, if they are hit here," pointing to the abdomen, "knock 'em on the head; they can't get well." The results in military surgery before the coming of Lister had shown no improvement since the days of Ambroise Paré (1517–90). A story is told that one day during a battle he saw three desperately wounded soldiers placed with their backs against a wall. An old campaigner inquired: "Can these fellows get well?" "No," answered Paré. Thereupon the old campaigner went up to them and cut all their throats "sweetly and without wrath" (*doucement et sans colère*).

No wonder that the public dreaded the mention of an operation, and shrank and shuddered at the suggestion of entering a hospital. Admission to a surgical ward was looked upon as the entrance to the valley of the shadow of death. Sir Frederick Treves used to tell how he had been deputed, when house-surgeon, to secure the consent of an East End mother for the admission of her daughter for some trifling operation. "That's all right," said the parent, "it's easy enough to give my consent, but what I want to know is—who's going to pay for the poor girl's funeral?"

Nor was the terror of death limited to surgical operations. It is not a century since Velpeau (1795–1867) said that "a pin-prick was a door for death." The heavy death-toll paid by parturient women is a tragic remembrance. In Buda-Pesth Lying-in Hospital the death-rate of 3–9 per cent. might at times reach a monthly average of 25–30 per cent. Yet when, after I had been house-surgeon to Lister, I became Resident Medical Officer at Queen Charlotte's Lying-In Hospital, and there introduced antiseptic methods, not a single mother or infant was lost during my term of office; a record, I believe, previously unknown in that institution.

But it is not only the security of surgical and obstetrical measures which is guaranteed to us by the work of Lister. Based on his principles the whole empire of medicine has been extended and consolidated. Listerism is the foundation of the vast edifice of hygiene and preventive medicine. The investigations leading to the discovery of the control of epidemic disease; the rapid disappearance of typhoid, cholera and plague ; the investigation of tropical diseases ; the establishment of blood transfusion and other remedial measures were made possible by the methods of Listerian surgery. The conquests of bacteriology, a subject unrecognised and untaught when Lister came to King's, were based on the confidence begotten of Lister's hard-won proof of the rightness of Pasteur's discoveries. Diseases which had previously vexed and ravaged mankind have been reduced to insignificance. Areas of the world which were the white man's grave, and districts where civilisation could never hope to penetrate, have been opened to commerce and even to pleasure-trippers.

Nowadays, what a miraculous change !

As Treves said of the surgical revolution of the Victorian period : " It is a question if any change in human affairs, or any disturbance in human creeds, has ever been so striking, so thorough, and so unexpected as has been this stirring crisis of the healing art."

The operative death-rate to-day is from 2 to 3 per cent., and this is practically made up of cases admitted almost moribund, such as advanced abdominal disease, and others operated on to relieve suffering, or with a faint hope of saving life. Our long waiting lists for admission demonstrate the different viewpoint of the public to-day. The safety of operative measures warranted their extension to formerly " untouchable " corners of the body. This extension has in these few decades been so rapid that Moynihan stated three years ago that " the craft of surgery has in truth nearly reached its limit in respect both of range and of safety." Lister's principles are so perfect in their simplicity that any house surgeon can to-day with confidence perform operations undreamt of when I was his dresser.

No longer is a pin-prick the door of death ; the cavities of the chest, abdomen and cranium are boldly opened for mere inspection; the wards no longer reek with the fœtor of putrefaction and sour poultices. The poor patient lays himself upon the operating table with the complete confidence and assurance that disasters are rare, and then only inevitable. What a change from the year when Simpson, of Edinburgh, said that "the man laid on an operating table in one of our surgical hospitals is exposed to more chances of death than the English soldier on the field at Waterloo."

Why did Lister succeed when so many generations had failed?

Lister succeeded because his methods were the fruit at once of both science and art; because he was trained in strict scientific doctrine; because he had a sincere love of his calling, a profound veneration for the sanctity of his profession, the warmest love and pity for humanity, wide imagination with a meticulous care of detail, and the patience, industry and courage which were firmly founded on his unshakable conviction in the everlasting soundness of his principles. Where others had attempted, Lister achieved; where others had failed, he succeeded. The result was the birth of a new medicine—the child of Science and of Art.

It is customary to divide the history of our world into the two periods—before and after Christ—B.C. and A.D. The history of medicine and of human suffering will always be divided into the times before and after the coming of Lister.

The hour had come; the man for it was ready to fill the unforgiving minute with sixty seconds' worth of distance run. He was able for it in many ways, but chiefly from the potent power of his personality. Another superman in a very different walk of life, viz., Beethoven, has recorded the following opinion: "I do not recognise any other sign of superiority but goodness." And he repeats:

"Where there is no great character, there is no great man." Anyone open to the greatness of a great soul could recognise, as the poet, W. E. Henley, did :

> "His faultless patience, his unyielding will,
> Beautiful gentleness and splendid skill."

Those who were Lister's immediate disciples all felt that he was powerful :

> "To compel
> Such love and faith as failure cannot quell."

And even those who were not his immediate followers came under the spell and realised, as Raymond Crawfurd has written, that : "It was not the first time in the World's History that providence, with purposeful wisdom, had chosen a man of superlative saintliness to be a medium of salvation to the world."

Lister now belongs to the ages.

S. T.

XVIII WILLIAM TURNER
(1832–1916)

ANATOMIST AND ADMINISTRATOR

The name of William Turner is worthily enrolled among the "Masters of Medicine." The justification of this is not found in any conspicuous single contribution which he made to the science of medicine. His name is not linked, like those of Addison, Bright and Stokes, with any form of disease which he was the first to recognise, or any notable symptom which he was the first to describe. Nor is it associated with researches bearing directly on the practice of medicine or surgery, like those of Horsley and Starling. His scientific life was devoted to Anatomy, and within that mother science mainly to physical anthropology, a subject which has little application to medical practice.

His eminence, and he held a very high place among his contemporaries, was due not only to his scientific work, but also to his influence on students as a teacher of anatomy, his work in administration for the development of the University of Edinburgh, of which he became the Principal, and to his distinction as President of the General Medical Council.

Turner was one of that fairly numerous band of Englishmen who, reversing the traditional stream of Scotsmen southwards, have crossed the Border in the opposite direction, settled down in the country of their adoption, and attained in Scotland to success and to lucrative posts of

SIR WILLIAM TURNER, K.C.B., M.B., LL.D., F.R.S.
1832–1916

To face p. 148

distinction. He was born in Lancaster, and throughout his whole life retained something of the pomposity of diction and expression which are said to characterise the speech of the natives of that town. His father died while still young, and, like Sir James Mackenzie [p. 214], he was apprenticed, while still a boy, though for only a very short time, to a pharmaceutical chemist. After serving for some years as apprentice to a practitioner in Lancaster, he went to London for his medical education, and was trained in St. Bartholomew's Hospital Medical School. For this school he retained permanently a great affection, as well as for Sir James Paget, who was one of his teachers, and for George Rolleston, a fellow student who was afterwards Linacre Professor of Anatomy and Physiology in the University of Oxford.

He was a good student, hard-working and successful in examinations, winning a scholarship at St. Bartholomew's and a gold medal at the University of London in Materia Medica and Pharmaceutical Chemistry. He had thoughts of becoming a chemist, and entered for a scholarship in chemistry, but was beaten in the examination by the son of a farmer, who had the advantage that a question had been set on agricultural chemistry. Before he had passed his final M.B. examination of London University the opportunity of work of a different kind was put before him.

John Goodsir, a famous anatomist in Edinburgh University, had been absent from his duties on account of his health for a year, and his classes had been taken by Dr. John Struthers, the extra-mural lecturer on anatomy in Edinburgh. When Goodsir returned to Edinburgh, in 1854, he found that he had no demonstrators, and no suitable candidates were to be found in Edinburgh. He turned to his old friend Sharpey, in University College,

London, and to Sir James Paget at St. Bartholomew's. Paget had known Turner for some years, and had in fact communicated to the Royal Society a paper by him on the chemical examination of cerebro-spinal fluid taken from a case of spina bifida treated by Paget. Turner, nearly ten years later, showed his interest in pathology, and his great admiration and respect for his friend, by revising and editing Paget's lectures on surgical pathology.

Goodsir interviewed Turner in London at his hotel, and tested him on the spot by asking him how he would describe the sartorius muscle, a question which evidently suited Turner, for Goodsir promptly invited him to take the post of senior demonstrator at a "liberal offer" of £200 a year, with the prospect of increase if he proved suitable.

The offer was accepted, Turner travelled north to Edinburgh—his first visit to it—in the autumn of 1854. Thus was begun a career which was to be devoted to the University of Edinburgh and its interests, and to the science of anatomy as demonstrator, for thirteen years, and as Professor from 1864 until 1903, when he was called to occupy the highest post the University could offer, that of Principal, and he occupied it until his death in 1916.

When he came to Edinburgh it was already a great medical school, attracting many students from a wide area. He was to see great changes and to participate in many of them. Anæsthetics had been introduced by Sir J. Y. Simpson [p. 124], but the antiseptic and aseptic eras of surgery were yet to come.

Anatomy was still in the revolution which followed the enunciation of the cell theory. There was to follow that period of feverish activity in which the histology of every tissue of the body was to be revolutionised. The structure of the nervous system was still to be unravelled, the story of human embryology to be unfolded, the chief discoveries about prehistoric man to be made, and the Darwinian theory of evolution to be enunciated.

On his arrival in Edinburgh, Turner found himself in a difficult environment. He had had little experience of anatomy—it had not been his principal work as a student—he had the demonstrations to prepare, he had some private coaching, he had still to pass the final M.B. examination of London University, and he had therefore little leisure. But he found his occupation full of interest. He was friendly to the students, and soon became very popular with them. He made the acquaintance of another young Englishman who had come up just before him to Edinburgh, whose name was to resound throughout all time as the greatest benefactor of the human race—Joseph Lister [p. 137]. For a time they worked together and published the results of their work on the structure of nerve fibres in a joint paper in 1855–6.

The next thirteen years of Turner's history was a period of great industry and activity. He wrote extensively, and his original work and publications, as well as his success as a teacher, made his name stand high among anatomists.

After a prolonged illness, Goodsir died in 1863, and the Chair of Anatomy in the University was vacant. There was a keen contest for it ; Turner had a hard fight against Struthers, but he was appointed, and as Professor he devoted himself more and more to the development and interests of the University.

This is not the occasion to describe fully or to discuss critically Turner's scientific work. Its scope was wide, within the bounds of anatomy. He wrote some 277 papers dealing with a great variety of subjects, but, naturally, the great majority of them were anatomical. He worked on the brain, topographically, and on the comparative anatomy of its convolutions. His work preceded that of Elliot Smith, in whose hands morphology and the study of function have been combined so as to afford some of the greatest advances ever made in neurology. Turner worked on the placenta, and he lived to appreciate the fresh light thrown on placental structure and function which was to follow from the study of its development in the hands of other workers.

He described many anatomical variations, and he was the first to describe, on the basis of a rare case of vascular obstruction, a "retroperitoneal anastomosis" between visceral and parietal branches of the abdominal aorta. He worked extensively on skulls and bones, applying the methods which had been recently introduced for this purpose by the great Paul Broca, and using as his material the large collections sent to Edinburgh on the return of the "Challenger" expedition, and also specimens sent to him from many parts of the world by old pupils. Later he became deeply interested in pre-history, and he wrote a very useful descriptive account of crania of the bronze age, and other pre-historic periods of Scotland.

He wrote on the anatomy of whales, and he dissected the famous Longniddry whale, a specimen of the "finner" species, over 80 feet long, which came ashore near Gulane, and slowly rotted away on the beach.

His work, as will be gathered, was almost purely descriptive. There was little original thought in his papers, but they form a storehouse of exact information on the topics with which they deal.

Turner was probably at his best in his cranial work. He loved the routine methods of making measurements and accumulating figures, from which he could construct averages for the whole series, for male and female specimens, and so on, though he never used the more modern methods of statistical enquiry which Karl Pearson was bringing into use.

A survey of Turner's work carries us a long way back into the last century. His name was widely known then both at home and abroad ; but since he resigned the Chair of Anatomy in Edinburgh in 1903, generation after generation of medical students has passed through its portals to whom, as well as to those of the present generation, Turner is a dim and remote figure.

Yet there are few whose influence and work are more deeply imprinted on the Edinburgh Medical School than his. His work persists in material things, for the buildings of the present medical school were erected in his time and under his guidance ; he planned the anatomy department, which is in use at the present time almost unchanged, and he was a sort of foster-father to the great McEwan Hall, for all the plans and the details for its construction passed through his hands. Equally noticeable, his influence is shown—*monumentum ære perennius*—in the tradition of lucid exposition and clear verbal demonstration which is handed down to every young demonstrator turned out from the school in which Turner displayed these gifts in so commanding a fashion.

My own first meeting with Turner, like that of so many others, was at his introductory lecture on anatomy to the first-year students. My acquaintance with him was to last for several years, for I was one of his demonstrators in the last years of his tenure of the Chair, until he was appointed Principal in 1903.

His appearance was impressive. It was difficult to think of him as the slim, fair-haired lad that he was when he came from London to be senior demonstrator to Goodsir. He was of medium height and burly, his movements active and alert : he looked as if he might have been an athlete in his younger days. He carried his head well, with an air of dignity. The lower part of his face was covered by a short white beard and moustache and side whiskers which passed into the profuse soft white hair of his temples. The vault of his head was rounded and dome-shaped. His nose was short with wide alæ; his blue eyes were small and deeply set, the surroundings full and a mass of wrinkles, and in the eyes there could be a delightful twinkle. His sententious manner gave impressiveness to his speech, and he could enunciate to his class, and even to a learned audience, commonplaces of anatomy in such a way as to give them the air of being original and novel. I have heard him, in the course of an address, tell the Royal Society of Edinburgh that "in the human manus are five digits," with such an air that one could almost hear some of the audience saying to themselves, "Well, I never realised that until now."

Turner excelled as a demonstrator of anatomy. His great success was due in part to his good, clear voice, his slow and impressive manner of speaking, but even more to the clearness and lucidity of his descriptions. He was at his best in his anatomical demonstrations. In his lectures dealing with systematic anatomy he was less successful in retaining the interest of the class. This was in no sense due to any weakness or incapacity on Turner's part, but solely from the nature of the matter dealt with. Pure descriptive anatomy apart from the discussion of function is not a subject suitable for systematic lectures, but Turner was slow to make any change in the instruction given from year to year. He inherited from Goodsir an arrangement of classes and a time-table of class hours, and he retained the arrangement and the time-table almost unchanged during practically the whole of his professoriate.

One part of the class work in anatomy made a great impression on students: it was a series of oral examinations which Turner conducted himself in the last year of the anatomy course. The senior class—it numbered over two hundred students—was divided into sections of from twenty to thirty, and an hour was set aside for each section at each examination period. The students were seated in a semi-circle behind a table, and Turner stood in the middle of the circle accompanied for many years by his well-known senior assistant, David Hepburn, who held the book in which marks were written down. There was great solemnity and gravity in the whole proceedings. First came a set of specimens of bones, whole or cut into artful fragments, and the professor handed round the box from which each student had to pick a specimen. Then each in turn was asked to name the specimen, no easy matter when only a fragment was provided, and to answer some fairly elementary question about it. Turner went round the whole circle, then turned to Hepburn and checked the marks which had been given. After one " round " or so Turner knew the name of every member.

After the bones had been dealt with came the muscles, nerves and blood vessels, and the same procedure was followed : Turner passing from one student to another and asking each a question on a dissected specimen. Again at the end of the round the marks were checked, and Turner could recollect every question which had been given to each student. When one section of the class was finished, another came on, and this work of oral examination went on for several hours for two or three days. The excitement among the candidates ran high—the examination was competitive, and each heard what the answers were of the other candidates, and knew how the marks stood. Seldom was a medal won with less than full marks in the series of examinations.

In the later years of his Professoriate he instituted a class of physical anthropology, and I attended one of the first of these courses. It formed an admirable introduction to the subject, and the wide range of specimens with which it was illustrated gave it great value. The skull specimens from the anatomical museum were in succeeding years to form the material for a classical treatise by Turner's distinguished son, Logan, on the air sinuses of the frontal bone.

The duties of the administrative work for the University in which Turner was immersed rendered it impossible for him to give to his department of anatomy all the attention he would have liked. Much had to be left to his assistants, and some of the newer and more vital aspects of anatomy were not cultivated as they were in other countries. At the same time it is only right to say that Turner was always appreciative and encouraging to any member of his staff who was prepared to work seriously along these lines by newer methods.

He did not himself make use of these methods, but worked on with the old ones with the help of his faithful laboratory assistants, of whom William Stirling was the first; and the little one-eyed man, Simpson, known to the students as "Cyclops," was the last.

No account of Turner would be adequate which failed to give some account of his more public work within the University and in the General Medical Council. He was noted for shrewdness and insight, and he gained and preserved the friendship and respect of his colleagues. He was asked to serve the University in many capacities, and in whatever capacity he served, the good work he did was recognised. He was for a time the Dean of the Medical Faculty, then he was elected an Assessor on the University Court, and as assessor or principal he sat for twenty-six years on the Court.

In Edinburgh many difficult questions had to be faced:

the extension of the medical buildings was urgently needed. Turner worked hard for this, and in time the University New Buildings, as they were termed, were erected. There were also the thorny problems of the relations of the Extra-Mural Medical Classes to the University, and, later, that of the admission of women to the University. In these, Turner's attitude was frankly conservative: he opposed the entrance of women, but he lived to see them in the University, and he accepted the situation.

He represented the Universities of Edinburgh and Aberdeen on the General Medical Council from November 1st, 1873, until December 4th, 1883, and the University of Edinburgh alone from December 18th, 1886. His capacity for business management, his clearness of vision and of expression, and his great sense of fairness, marked him out among his colleagues. When Sir Richard Quain, the President, died in 1898, Turner was elected to be his successor.

Turner's scientific work is recorded in his numerous publications, and his work for the University and for medical education lives in the walls of the University itself. It is less easy to describe the personal qualities which were behind his work, and the sort of impression he made on his fellows. Turner was greatly respected, greatly liked, and it is not too much to say he was perhaps a good deal held in awe. I owe much to Turner, and I can appreciate the admirable account of this side of Turner's character given in the excellent biography of his father, prepared in filial respect by a devoted and distinguished son, who has himself inherited many of those mental qualities which characterised his father.[1]

A vivid picture of Turner has recently been given by

[1] "Sir William Turner: A Chapter in Medical History." A. Logan Turner.

his distinguished student, Professor D'Arcy Thompson, in an address to the Royal Society of Edinburgh, and these memories will re-echo in the minds of many of Turner's former students.[1]

"Turner lived so long that we can all remember him: his sturdy figure, his rapid walk, his little shake of the head, the twinkle of his eye, his dominant personality. He was a trifle pompous sometimes, and fond of the old verbiage of the anatomists. He came along when I was doing my first day's work in the old dissecting room. 'Well, what have you got?' said he. 'An arm, sir,' said I, very timidly. 'Call it a superior extremity; it's so much more precise!' And so indeed it was, from the point of view of the anatomist. As a demonstrator he was superb. One did not forget one's lesson in a hurry, when Turner had held up nerve or artery in his forceps, and told their names with such a look and voice as though the world depended on them. Of the papers which he read before our Society, many were about whales, for he inherited from Knox and Goodsir a lifelong interest in these great beasts, and an insatiable desire to add one after another to his fine collection. Turner had none of the poetry, scientific imagination or prophetic insight of Goodsir. But there was nothing Turner touched that he did not do with all his might; his love of his subject, his faith and enthusiasm, never flagged for a moment. He was a teacher and a master of men. He fairly won and manifestly deserved the honours that were heaped upon him."

D. W.

[1] "Fifty Years Ago in the Royal Society of Edinburgh," *Proc. Roy. Soc. of Edin.*, vol. liv, part 2.

HUGH OWEN THOMAS
1834–1891
(From " Hugh Owen Thomas—A Personal Study," by Frederick Watson)

To face p. 159

XIX HUGH OWEN THOMAS
(1834–1891)
ORTHOPÆDIC SURGEON

A PLACE among the British Masters of Medicine is only to be accorded to those whose life and work has contributed something entirely new to our knowledge, such as Jenner's discovery that cow-pox affords an immunity from smallpox, or to those who give a new interpretation to the meaning of diseases or disorders of the human body, as was done by Sir James Mackenzie [p. 214], who, from his personal observation of cases met in a busy general practice in Burnley, evolved new interpretations of the meaning of "heart disease," and put the treatment of cardiac disorders on a completely new footing.

Hugh Owen Thomas was a "club doctor" in general practice in the slums near the docks in Liverpool. His patients were dock labourers and boiler-makers, painters and riggers, sea captains and common seamen : rough people, whose ordinary vocations involved risk to life and limb, and whose methods of settling their differences afforded Thomas many opportunities of treating fractures of the jaw. In 1867 he published an article on "Operative Treatment of Fractures of the Lower Jaw," which was quoted in Bryant's "Practice of Surgery" as being a new procedure. It consisted in wiring the teeth together, much as the dentist does to-day, or in drilling the bones and wiring them together ; but Thomas twisted each end of the wire separately into a flat spiral which lay against the gum, causing no irritation to the cheek or lip. I first saw this method employed by Sir Robert Jones [p. 176] over thirty years ago, when I was house-surgeon, and was surprised at the comfort of the patient. Thomas also pointed out that if the root of a displaced tooth presented in the fracture, it would delay union and should be extracted. This is a point which was specially noted during the treatment of such cases in the Great War.

Sir Robert Jones, in his Presidential Address in 1913, when he described Owen Thomas's treatment of intestinal disease and obstruction, and again in the first Thomas Memorial Lecture, founded by the Liverpool Medical Institution in 1922, thirty-one years after Thomas died, gives an intimate personal description of Thomas and his work which only he could have described. For in 1873 Sir Robert Jones was apprenticed to Owen Thomas, and lived in his house, while attending the Medical School in Liverpool. It was his intention, had he lived, to publish a biography of Owen Thomas in the centenary year of his birth. This task has been undertaken by the biographer of Sir Robert Jones. I have been privileged to assist on the surgical side, and have had access to early manuscript notes of Thomas's cases, which show that within ten years from the time he became a Member of the College of Surgeons, in 1857, he had evolved fundamental conservative principles of treatment by rest and protection from injury, not merely for limbs, but for acute abdominal lesions. In the case of limbs, he invented splints to put his principles effectively into practice. In the case of the acute abdominal lesions, he laid down treatment and dietary almost identical with that laid down in *The Practitioner* for 1933, for similar conditions, with this difference, that, in 1875, when Thomas first wrote on the acute abdomen, which he called obstruction, there was little differential diagnosis, and enterotomy was the only recognised abdominal operation.

Owen Thomas in his day and generation was a sagacious and observant physician, but he is remembered more as the founder in this country of conservative principles and methods of treatment of lesions of bones and joints, which have been enlarged by Robert Jones, and transmitted to us in the present day, to form the foundations of our British school of orthopædic practice. No surgeon can become really great unless he be a sound physician, although any mechanically-minded person can by practice become an efficient operator. Thomas, in his own writings, proves himself master both of the "Art of Medicine and of the Craft of Surgery."

Now Hugh Owen Thomas was the son of a bone-setter who practised in the same district of Liverpool in which his son afterwards lived and practised. Moreover, Evan Thomas, the father, was the seventh bone-setter in lineal descent, the previous six having been farmers in Anglesey who also practised the art of dealing with injuries. There is no doubt that they were held in high esteem, for one evening Sir Robert Jones showed me a series of cuttings from old newspapers extolling the services rendered by various generations of this family, and their virtues have been recorded in Welsh song. They appear occasionally to have accepted fees for their services, but they did not charge fees. They were primarily farmers, and such skill as lay in their hands was at the service of their neighbours, and regarded as a gift from God.

Evan Thomas went to Liverpool, and definitely practised as a bone-setter, or "irregular practitioner," which was the phrase used before the Medical Act of 1858 defined a "qualified practitioner." This Evan Thomas was a tall man, over six feet in height, austere and strict in his habits, official referee to several workmen's clubs and tontines, and recognised as being successful in his treatment of fractures, dislocations and injuries. Sir Robert Jones records that Owen Thomas told him his father was not rough in his methods; he used a great deal of power in the form of traction, if necessary to reduce a deformity, but it was always uniform and never spasmodic. Owen Thomas was only five feet four, a delicate boy, who at the age of seventeen was apprenticed to his maternal uncle, Dr. Roberts, of St. Asaph.

Dr. Roberts was a scholarly man, who not only prepared his pupil for study at Edinburgh, but did much to foster in him the instincts of a student. In 1855 Owen Thomas went to Edinburgh for two years, and, after a further year of study in London, became a Member of the Royal College of Surgeons in 1857. After a short visit to Paris, where he seems to have been greatly interested in various patterns of lithotrites, he returned to assist his father, who had been in practice in Liverpool since 1831, and was therefore well established, although he held no diploma. The first Medical Act of 1858 was imminent, however, and on January 1st, 1859, the first register appeared, with the name of Hugh Owen Thomas duly registered with the Diploma of M.R.C.S. The old bone-setter had evidently noted the signs of the times, and recognised that the days were passing when the medical practitioner sought the aid of the handicraft of the bone-setter; he therefore sent his five sons to Edinburgh to obtain "registrable qualifications." The story of those troubled times is told in the account of Hugh Owen Thomas. His father was tried at Chester Assizes in 1860, on a charge of manslaughter. The Judge suggested an element of malice in the prosecution. Hugh, who had attended the case with his father, gave evidence, and "the Senior Surgeon to the

Medical School in Liverpool" also gave evidence in his favour, and was found in fault by his colleagues for giving countenance to a bone-setter. There was a complete acquittal, and on his return Evan Thomas was given a triumphal reception by his patients and friends.

This was all very well for the father, but what about the lad Hugh, M.R.C.S., who had been writing to his former teachers, Hughes Bennett and John Struthers, about the proper way to become F.R.C.S.Ed.? This was no fit introduction to the professional world he sought to enter. His brother John escaped to the South of England, where his merits brought him distinction as a gynæcologist. On Hugh, the puny creature of 5 ft. 4 in., for whom his six-foot father perhaps saw little hope, descended the mantle of his bone-setting forefathers. His destiny was to combine this hereditary craft with the knowledge gained in the medical schools, and thus to lay the foundations of orthopædic practice on which Robert Jones has built so much. When his father retired in 1863, his clubs and the allegiance of his patients passed to Owen Thomas, but he received no goodwill, and no support from the profession in Liverpool.

For the first fifteen years of his professional life Thomas must have led a very lonely existence, for he was cut off from the academic side of surgical life by reason of his association with his father, and probably also on account of his eccentricity in dress. He always wore a nautical cap, with the peak pulled down to shade an eye which had been injured by a stone in boyhood; he also wore a frock coat, closely buttoned to the neck, showing no trace of linen or collar, probably to keep his frail body warm. Nevertheless, in 1864, he married Elizabeth Jones, Robert Jones's aunt, "a beautiful and charming woman." Music and working at his lathe, designing and making splints, were his only recreations. Mrs. Thomas has recorded that in the whole of his married life Thomas only spent six nights away from home. He must have realised early that he had no prospect of an appointment on a hospital staff. He was, however, not one to be denied the opportunity to work, for his work was his life. He treated his patients in their own homes, and very soon had a private hospital of his own. His " new hospital, at 28 Hardy Street," was opened in March, 1872, and the Admission Book and Register, covering a number of years, have been preserved. Of his former hospital no record remains except one reference : for " Geo. Davies," one of the first patients admitted to the new hospital, " was operated on in my old hospital in Greta Street." This was a successful operation on an old case of ununited fracture of the humerus, with a result of which those of us who worked on such cases in the War would not have been ashamed.

Apart from his printed work and a personal knowledge of his methods contributed by Sir Robert Jones and John Ridlon, who first met Thomas in 1887, we have as available material for re-discovering the working of Thomas's mind, his case-book, which commences in May, 1857, when he was helping his father, Evan Thomas. In this book we have, first, records of cases which interested him in his father's practice, such as a dislocation of the shoulder which occurred on January 25th, 1855, off the Cape of Good Hope, and was successfully reduced by Evan Thomas twenty months later, on October 31st, 1857, without anæsthetic and without fracturing the neck of the humerus ; the result was so good that Hugh had photographs taken, but these, alas ! are lost. There is a brief interval after Thomas started his independent practice in 1859, presumably until he found his feet and launched out on surgical work. About 1864 he performed his first operation for fracture of the jaw. In his later writings on fractures he tells us that in his early days he used wooden splints, and for fractured femurs the long Liston splint. From the case-book we find that he finally abandoned the long Liston splint in January, 1867, and in September of the same year Sara McTurc was the first patient ever treated on a Thomas hip splint. This is an amazing record when one thinks that Hugh Owen Thomas did all this in the ten years from the time he became M.R.C.S., and until Evan Thomas retired, in 1863, he stood by his old father and his bone-setting practice. When we come to the Register of the New Hospital in Hardy Street, we get new little revelations. This is not a case-book, but merely a record of names, addresses and dates. Opposite each case, however, there is a small sketch of the splints used for primary treatment, or of the splints worn when the patient was discharged. Thus, opposite a case of Pott's fracture there is a little diagram of an outside iron with inside T-strap to prevent recurrence of the valgus deformity. The importance of this is now known at least to orthopædic surgeons. When Thomas wrote in the *Provincial Medical Journal* of 1888 (Vol. VII, p. 355), on fractures, particularly Colles's fracture of the radius and Pott's fracture of the fibula, he explained that the irregular practitioners whom he had met in his youth reduced these fractures as well as any surgeon, but in the case of the latter injury (Pott's fracture) they often failed from want of centralising the foot afterwards. This was printed without any explanation or diagram of what he meant by centralising the foot. To those of us who have been trained by Robert Jones, and to our pupils, the meaning is obvious. To us it means that the sole of the foot must be kept near the middle line of the body, to avoid the risk of a " valgus " strain on the callus when walking is commenced. I have purposely used the words "valgus" strain, for I am conscious that I often use it when demonstrating cases in my wards. Such a phrase conveys no very clear message to a reader, but is quite clear if the teacher demonstrates his meaning by action. The craft of orthopædic manipulations and of the proper way to use splints can only be taught by practical demonstration, not by written descriptions. Thomas had no students to teach. If it had not been for Sir Robert Jones, his one real disciple who had a long training in his craft, this would have been lost to us. There was more to be learned by watching Robert Jones's hands than from anything he said or wrote if one had not seen those wonderful hands at work.

In 1875 Thomas began publishing. All his material for publication was already formulated. Theories regarding the physiological nature of disease, principles of treatment, also based on physiology, and diet, splints and general management of the case to give effect to those principles, were ordered and arranged in Thomas's mind during those first fifteen years of slum practice. His methods were not those taught in the schools of his day; these he had tried and found wanting. Time and riper experience show that what Thomas rejected is dead, but what he tried to teach has survived both in the treatment of ulcers and inflammation of the alimentary tract and in his principles and methods of treatment of bones and joints.

Professor Rushton Parker was the only medical man of standing in Liverpool who ever gave Thomas any open support or countenance. Their first meeting was casual, for Dr. Parker senior, as police surgeon, had to see Thomas about a police inspector with a fractured leg who was under Thomas's care, and young Rushton, then demonstrator of anatomy, accompanied his father. Rushton

Parker, as will be told [p. 174], has recorded that he was so struck with the arrangements for the comfort of the patients and with the beautiful control of limbs by various splints of novel design, that he urged Thomas to publish without delay. Rushton Parker immediately introduced Thomas's methods in his wards, and remained an active supporter and staunch friend to the end of his life, at some real risk to his own prospects of advancement.

Thomas had never served an apprenticeship in the art of teaching or of writing lectures so ordered that students could easily follow the main principles of treatment. He had never been house-surgeon or surgical tutor, and had never been subject to the discipline of being an assistant surgeon and of having to subordinate his own ideas and methods to the rules of treatment laid down by his senior surgeon. Except for eighteen months with his father, Thomas had been his own master ; for him a text-book was not an authority to be followed, but something to be criticised and tested by clinical experience. All Thomas's books were privately printed at his own expense, and were not issued by a publishing house, therefore few copies can have been sold by booksellers. Thomas sent copies gratis to surgeons all over the world, and immediately sent them to anybody who enquired where they were to be obtained. It is small wonder that he failed to reach the medical public of his day ; only those who visited him and saw him at work could really appreciate what Thomas was doing. Although letters received by him show that he was often invited to address medical societies, there are no records of his having done so except on two occasions. The first was during the Liverpool meeting of the British Medical Association in 1883, when he gave a demonstration of cases in his own house, duly reported in the Journal [1883, ii, 324] ; the second was in May, 1887, when he addressed the Harveian Society in London, when Edmund Owen was President.

We must not forget that Thomas was a general practitioner. His first round of visits started before 6 a.m. Sometimes when he knocked at the door a hand would appear with a milk jug. He made his evening visits to dangerous cases of pneumonia or acute abdominal cases after dinner. About ten o'clock at night he sat down to enter up his notes and write his books. On Sundays he saw poor patients free in his own house, to which he had built an annexe like the out-patient department of a small hospital. He looked forward to Sunday evening, when Mrs. Thomas played the piano and sang, while he played the accompaniment on a flute—his only relaxation.

The first book, written in 1875 at the instigation of Rushton Parker and published within the year, dealt with the treatment of diseases of hip-, knee- and ankle-joints. The book immediately aroused interest. Early in 1876 Thiersch wrote from Germany for samples of the splints; Taylor, from America, protested that Thomas misunderstood his teaching; early in 1877 Howard Marsh described the Thomas splint as the best yet devised for controlling the hip-joint, though he still preferred weight-and-pulley traction for reducing deformity in the first instance. In 1878 Edmund Owen wrote urging Thomas to attend the British Medical Association at Bath, and personally demonstrate his doctrines. In 1879 the organising secretary of the meeting in Cork invited him to go there, yet Thomas stayed in Liverpool, and the discussion on hip disease was opened by Sayre from America. Nothing could tear Thomas from his practice, which he had conducted single-handed for so long that he could not leave it even for a few days. This is the great tragedy of Thomas's life. If at that moment he had attended meetings of the British

Medical Association, the intense earnestness of the man, the soundness of his logic, the ingenuity with which he had devised splints to give practical effect to the faith that was in him, would have revealed to the medical world that in Liverpool there was a prophet whose message was at least worthy of consideration. " There is a tide in the affairs of men," and Thomas, the recluse, missed his flood-tide. It took Robert Jones a lifetime of patient unobtrusive precept and example to establish principles which Thomas, in his generation, failed to establish.

In 1875, when this book on " Diseases of Joints " was written, Thomas also wrote an article on the past and present treatment of Intestinal Obstructions, which appeared in the *Liverpool and Manchester Medical and Surgical Reports for* 1877 [published in 1878, p. 1].

When, in 1883, Thomas planned a book which was ultimately to take form as a sort of system of treatment, he gave precedence to the " Treatment of Intestinal Diseases and Obstruction," which was published as Part I of " Contributions to Medicine and Surgery." The attitude of his mind towards inflammation and disease in general is shown more clearly in this book than in any other. He followed Hilton's teaching in " Rest and Pain," but was much more rigorous and exacting than Hilton ever was in the measures he adopted to enforce rest. In the first place Thomas recognised that an inflamed tissue could not perform its usual function ; second, that the symptoms arising from the inflammation indicated the course to be taken by the physician. Thus, he recognised that with the onset of inflammation in a joint the earliest symptom was a contraction of the surrounding muscles. This Thomas interpreted as a protective reflex effort to put the joint at rest, hence his splints, designed to assist nature by providing mechanical rest, thus allowing the muscles to relax, for there was no reflex call on their activity. In the case of lesions of the intestines, loss of appetite and, still more, vomiting were direct indications that no food was required.

In developing his argument, Thomas took typhoid fever as an example of ulceration, and recognised that, as a specific fever, it must run its allotted course, which no known treatment could shorten, but erratic or ill-considered diet might make the condition worse. Mrs. Thomas has told us that Thomas, in discussions round the dinner table, "liked an opponent better than one who agreed with him." In his writings, Thomas almost invariably took some published work as an opponent against which to argue, and by argument to prove his points. Thus, in his discussion of typhoid fever, he took an able lecture by Sir William Jenner, published in *The Lancet* [1879, ii, p. 715], as an object of attack. After acknowledging the precision with which the various points had been stated, Thomas proceeds to dissect the lecture section by section. Diet: It was acknowledged that milk must be used with care. Diarrhœa: Examine the stools for milk curds. Hæmorrhage: Stop milk; administer opium. Perforation: Still more alarming. Thomas argued: If milk is so dangerous, why use it at all? An inflamed bowel cannot digest, therefore give it nothing but water to quench thirst, and let it rest and heal. So he laid down, sixty years ago, a regime as strict as any I have met since, more strict than that taught me as a student.

In his general practice, Thomas met many cases of "intestinal obstruction." In his day the routine treatment was enormous doses of castor oil, croton oil, and enemata. If a lump was felt in the abdomen it was often kneaded. Such treatment violated Thomas's principles of rest. Thomas was quite alive to the possibilities of operation, for he reported [*The Lancet*, 1875, ii, p. 877] three cases of operative treatment of intussusception by London surgeons, two of which were successful. Commenting on the report of the discussion, Thomas pointed out that the difficulty and danger of the operation had been increased by the previous use of drastic purges for several days, and complained most bitterly that of the ten eminent men who discussed the case, not one found fault with the preliminary treatment by aperients and taxis. Space does not permit a detailed description of Thomas's plan for treating intestinal lesions. It consisted in raising the foot of the bed; aperients and enemata were avoided because they excited peristalsis—on this point he is very insistent—opium, if necessary, to allay pain; paracentesis of the bowel if distended by gas; enterotomy he occasionally performed. Above all, a regulated diet during convalescence and a strict diet for some months after was rigidly enforced.

In Treves's Jacksonian Essay on "Intestinal Obstruction," statistics showed a mortality of 53 per cent. in cases of enterotomy for all cases of obstruction, excluding intussusception and malignant disease. Laparotomy for intussusception was attended by a mortality of 72 per cent.

Thomas's treatment when he encountered an acute abdominal case, followed by pain, vomiting and perhaps at first diarrhœa, followed by a complete constipation, was to regard this as an acute inflammation requiring immediate physiological rest. When the symptoms abated the first diet he allowed was water arrowroot. Case after case is recorded where, after days of stercoraceous vomiting, flatus was passed perhaps on the seventeenth day, and the bowels acted on the twenty-third day. As was recorded in "Case 19," which was attended in 1878 by Thomas and Robert Jones, a hundred visits were paid in the course of thirty days. Every detail of Thomas's regimen and diet reappears, in 1902, in Ochsener's treatment for cases of appendicitis which were too inflamed for immediate operation, and Ochsener claimed that 90 per cent. of cases with localised peritonitis shutting off an appendix which was perhaps perforated, could be carried through successfully until an operation could be performed in the resting stage. There is no doubt that Thomas, by his careful regimen, successfully treated what he called typhlitis, intussusception, and some cases which he vaguely diagnosed as enteritis or ulcers. His object in writing was to try to get this treatment taught to the general practitioners. Papers and articles in *The Practitioner* [1933, Vol. 131, p. 353], by Hurst, on the medical treatment of gastric and duodenal ulcers, and by Melly, on certain cases of appendicitis, practically repeated what Thomas taught fifty years before. That the diet suitable in the first week of the treatment of an ulcer is the correct treatment until the ulcer is healed, was part of Thomas's creed, as it is to-day the teaching of Dr. Hurst.

In the realm of surgery Thomas was always interested in lithotomy, and designed a special staff and director for the perineal operation which is no longer of any interest. His treatment of joints was founded on the same principles of complete physiological rest, as was his treatment of acute intestinal lesions. For hip disease, the splints used in his day were all lateral splints applied to the side of the limb and body. In such splints the hip sagged and moved if the patient was lifted for nursing purposes, therefore Thomas had to design a *posterior* splint to stop this movement. The principle of the splint was due to clinical acumen, the simplicity of the design to mechanical genius.

The Thomas knee splint was in the same way designed to give full control of the knee-joint, for it extended from the groin to the foot, and prevented movement at the knee-joint without the need for any sort of bandage on the inflamed joint. Thomas regarded inflammation as a physiological process of repair, demanding absolute freedom for the circulation of blood and lymph. Therefore he opposed the use of bandages round an "inflamed" area, and objected strongly to continued tension by weight and pulley, for the circulation cannot be perfectly free in tissues which are kept in a state of tension. Finally, distension of a joint by fluid exercised pressure on the synovial membrane and put tension on the capsule, and therefore he aspirated distended joints to avoid this injurious interference with normal physiological circulation of blood and lymph.

There is no need to enumerate his splints, as they are now well known in the world of surgery. Thomas's test of soundness in a healed joint was a new contribution to clinical lore. For example, a diseased elbow which had been kept flexed with the hand slung under the chin for months, or even years, might show no signs of active disease. On relaxing the sling some movement might be present. The sling was then relaxed two inches, and the patient told to practise movement. If at the end of three days this movement remained free, the joint was probably "sound," and a small further range of movement was allowed. If pain or stiffness occurred, the joint was not sound. Similarly, an anchylosed knee was tested by allowing the patient to walk without a guarding splint; if any deformity such as flexion occurred the anchylosis was unsound, and the splint was immediately applied again. In spite of the help given by X-rays this test remains as a necessary part of clinical technique. No such tests of clinical soundness had been formulated before it was laid down by Thomas. Similarly, in intestinal lesions, a clean tongue with the return of appetite and the sense of taste was an indication of recovery, and showed that complete starvation was no longer necessary. There is a strict logical continuity of fundamental principles in all Thomas's teaching.

Since the Great War Thomas's name has become famous because, as a direct consequence of the fact that after the R.A.M.C. stretcher bearers had been systematically taught how to fix compound fractures of the femur in Thomas's knee splint on the field, the death-rate arising from this injury fell from 80 per cent. to 20 per cent. This result was achieved because the pain, shock and, further, the spread of infection and inflammation were diminished by fixing the limb efficiently, so that injurious movement of injured tissues during transport was reduced to a minimum ; the splint was the simple means by which this could be done. Rushton Parker, describing his first visit to see the policeman in Thomas's "hospital," in 1875, wrote : "A police inspector suffering from compound fracture of the leg : I was struck with admiration at the apparatus slung from a crane in the man's bedroom, which kept the limb straight and still, with the wound clean and exposing a bare piece of the tibia. The limb was between parallel steel bars, fixed immovably and painlessly, the only dressing being occasional irrigation with water, but no covering of rag on the wound." An entry in the note-book about this time shows that Thomas used salt solution, not pure water, for irrigation in what he called the "open treatment." Similar treatment was in regular use by Robert Jones when I was his house-surgeon, but it took the dire needs of a Great War, in addition to the example and prestige of Sir Robert, to bring such methods back into practice.

Thomas is not to be remembered because he invented splints. It was his passion for knowledge, his recognition of physiological principles of tissue life and repair, that made him seek fundamental principles of treatment, logically carrying out the principles of physiological rest, which drove him to reduce the management of disease to a formula, and drove him to design splints to achieve his purpose with efficiency.

D. McC. A.

XX ROBERT JONES
(1857–1933)

MODERN ORTHOPÆDICS

It is impossible for the contemporaries, especially the friends, of a very distinguished man to determine his true and final place in history. Remote posterity, with which the decision rests, is concerned, however, with the deeds that live after him, and is interested in his character and individuality only in so far as they give clues to the principles and forces that activated his genius. On the other hand, those who have been associated with the man himself may be swayed by the memory of his compelling force or of the persuasive and popular appeal of his personality, and may find it hard to disentangle the features which are likely to have a permanent place in the chronicles of the subject he adorned from his personal glamour—the disciple-linked genes that will be transmitted for all time—from those which belong to his ancestors, to himself, and to his progeny.

Robert Jones,[1] the son of an imaginative, temperamental and perhaps somewhat feckless father, who was a journalist, must have derived from his mother the necessary counterpoise, without which he would probably never have succeeded in harnessing his thoughts to practical issues—an

[1] An interesting "Life of Robert Jones," written by his son-in-law, Mr. Frederick Watson, has been published by Messrs. Hodder & Stoughton, London, 1934. The present study was written in August, 1934.

1857–1933

Robert Jones in the uniform of a Major-General A.M.S., from a photograph taken in 1927.

To face p. 176

association which was so outstanding a factor in the success of his life work.

In this brief study of an extremely active, versatile, long and fruitful life, it will be best to try to draw a composite sketch, as it were, of the circumstances, characteristics and activities of Robert Jones, in an attempt to discern how he came to be the embodiment of all that is best in a medical man—a master of his craft, an inspiration to his disciples, a beloved and trusted healer of his fellow men.

That Robert Jones was a master surgeon—and this admits of no doubt—does not seem to have occurred for many years to his colleagues outside the wards of his own hospital, the Royal Southern, in Liverpool. Probably most of the surgeons in his own city before about the year 1900 would have dismissed the subject with the comment that he was a " good man with fractures and joints " ; in London he was regarded with suspicion as being related to bone-setters,[1] if, indeed, he was not one himself, such was the ignorance prevailing in the earlier years of his career.

No doubt that great pioneer of orthopædic surgery, Hugh Owen Thomas [p. 159], indirectly made the immediate acceptance of Robert Jones difficult, for his confidence in his own methods and his inability to suffer fools at all did not cause Thomas to be regarded with affection in Liverpool, and he was little known outside.

Thomas in himself, however, contained all the elements of greatness, and can stand alone in the Hall of Fame ; yet some have said that Hugh Owen Thomas's greatest contribution to surgery was Robert Jones. It may well be that the aphorism is more trite than true : this depends on the interpretation put upon it. In all probability Thomas did not perform " open " orthopædic operations ; but that

[1] Evan Thomas, the father of H. O. Thomas, was a bone-setter.

is not surprising, for he worked before and in the early days of antisepsis. Still, his vehement opposition to the prevalent and indiscriminate excision of joints was based on surgical judgment and not on the fear of sepsis. Robert Jones, while adopting the views of Thomas in regard to tuberculous joints in children, and his conservative orthopædic methods generally, became a pioneer of active surgical intervention when this was indicated. Yet history will almost certainly decide that Hugh Owen Thomas was as great, if not a greater, orthopædic figure ; an original thinker, austere and self-contained, caring nothing for bitter criticism beyond the opportunity it gave him of pouring out invective against the unbelievers, and ploughing his lonely professional furrow unfavoured by the gods.[1]

Such a career as that of Thomas would have been foreign to Robert Jones's disposition ; indeed, all who knew him most intimately must feel that had there been no Hugh Owen Thomas probably there would have been no orthopædic surgeon, Robert Jones.

It is difficult to believe that Robert Jones's mind and inclinations would have enabled him to become other than a popular and successful general surgeon, had he been obliged to carve his own career ; perhaps he would not have been a medical man at all. Be this as it may, from fifteen years of age Robert Jones was under the influence of that dominant character, Hugh Owen Thomas ; and as a young practitioner he became equipped, far in advance of any other surgeon in the country, for the type of work

[1] Excellent short accounts, however, of H. O. Thomas and his work may be found in the first Thomas Memorial Lecture, Liverpool Medical Institution (1922), by Sir Robert Jones, and in " Menders of the Maimed " (1919), by Sir Arthur Keith. A book entitled " Hugh Owen Thomas : a Personal Study," by Frederick Watson, was published in 1934.

to which he had been apprenticed. It has, on the other hand, required the prestige of Robert Jones to justify the work of Thomas, and to place on a pedestal of everlasting fame the uncle by marriage only,[1] with whom Robert Jones worked so long and whom he succeeded.

In this way Robert Jones, perhaps unknowingly, has well and truly repaid the debt he owed to his illustrious predecessor, Hugh Owen Thomas.

It is interesting to note that the year of grace 1934 was the centenary of the birth of Hugh Owen Thomas and also that of the Medical School of Liverpool. It will, therefore, not be inappropriate first to consider the relationship of these two men, whom it is hard to dissociate, to the chief institutions in their own city.

The principal medical societies were, and still are, the Liverpool Medical Institution, which sprang from the Medical Library founded in the year 1777, and the Medical and Literary Society, of which Robert Jones was one of the founders in 1884. In this latter Society, to which election is by invitation, Thomas, who was asked to join, found an admirable field, beyond the bounds of medicine, for the exercise of his dialectic faculties, which Robert Jones at that time undoubtedly shared in no mean degree. Although a member of the Liverpool Medical Institution from 1876 until his death in 1891, Thomas did not find this Society so congenial; but there Robert Jones, who was elected a member in 1883, brought the fruits of his experience on many occasions. He became a most popular and honoured president in the years 1912 and 1913; and in 1932 he celebrated the jubilee of his membership, having the year before received the distinction—unique for a member of the Institution in modern times—of

[1] H. O. Thomas married the sister of Robert Jones's father, and there was, therefore, no blood-relationship between the two surgeons.

honorary membership. Here it was, in the autumn of 1932, that he took part in a discussion for the last time, and made his last pronouncement on orthopædic surgery.

Meanwhile, Robert Jones had slowly climbed the ladder to professional success. In 1881 he had been appointed Honorary Assistant Surgeon to the Stanley Hospital, and in the same year, while still a young man, thirty-one years of age, he was made Surgeon-in-Chief to the Manchester Ship Canal, which was then being constructed. Here, during a period of five years, he was responsible for the treatment of a very large number and variety of accidents, the vast majority of which were orthopædic in character. In 1889, reversing an unfavourable decision given seven years previously, the committee elected Robert Jones an Honorary Surgeon to the Royal Southern Hospital, to which he was to bring great renown, and where he remained until the year 1917, when he retired under the age-limit regulation. For many years he had as a colleague William Alexander, a pioneer of gynæcological surgery, and also for a time one of the greatest of modern general surgeons, Frank T. Paul, and the doyen of radiology in this country, C. Thurstan Holland. The last two were subsequently elected to the active staff of the Royal Infirmary.

What did the Medical School of Liverpool do for the two makers of orthopædic surgery? H. O. Thomas was without a hospital appointment, his work being centred entirely in his private practice and his patients who attended his free clinics held on Sundays in his private house. He never came in touch with medical students; he left behind him no disciple whom he had trained, saving only Robert Jones, who also until his later years remained outside the inner academic circle. True, Robert Jones, in virtue of his hospital appointment, was for eleven years a member of the Clinical School, an amalgamation of the four principal hospitals in the city, which came into being in the year 1906; but it had then no official representative in the Faculty of Medicine. Previously the Royal Infirmary alone had been the clinical school for medical students, and it has always remained the chief centre of clinical education.

In 1918 the University of Liverpool, which in 1903 had severed its collegial association with the Victoria University of Liverpool and Manchester, accepted the endowment by Mr. John Rankin of a Lady Jones Lectureship in orthopædic surgery, and from 1919 to 1925 Robert Jones was honorary lecturer. From 1921 to 1932 he was Director of the Board of Orthopædic Studies in the University, with a seat in the Medical Faculty.

The degree of Mastership of Orthopædic Surgery, the first of its kind, was established in 1926, and Robert Jones became university lecturer; but it is to be doubted whether many students other than those who took the post-graduate course for the M.Ch. (Orth.) came under his influence. Vision must have been lacking and enthusiasm among the general surgeons absent, otherwise the young university would surely never have overlooked the advantages which would have accrued to it from the appointment of so great a man to its professorial staff. He himself had no personal ambitions in this direction, and certainly would have accepted no emoluments. Still, when the matter came up in conversation, he showed how much he would have appreciated this academic recognition. What an influence his charm, understanding, and simplicity would have had on those he taught.

In 1918 the Committee of the Royal Infirmary, on the recommendation of the medical staff, elected Robert Jones, Honorary Consulting Orthopædic Surgeon, a similar acknowledgment of his surgical standing being made by St. Thomas's Hospital, London. Both offices were sinecures, and reflected as much honour on the institutions concerned as on the man himself.

Recognition had, then, attended the footsteps of Robert Jones somewhat tardily. He must, however, have been too busy to reflect on such matters ; in any case he was always totally devoid of self-consciousness, self-glorification, and self-advancement. The time came, nevertheless, when even his own townsmen and countrymen could not remain deaf to the plaudits of his colleagues in both hemispheres, or blind to the number of eminent foreigners who thronged his clinics and were received with such hospitality in his home.

The Mayos and other eminent men from America, Mark Jansen, of Leiden, and a host of European surgeons had written ardent descriptions of his skill, and all the while Robert Jones had remained his modest, natural self. On one occasion when he gave a large dinner to about one hundred orthopædic surgeons and their wives, speech followed speech in his praise, and at last he leant across to a friend and said : "Is not this too dreadful ; whatever am I to say ?" He never thought back to the days when there had been so little acknowledgment of his work by his own people ; and he always, eagerly as a child, and gratefully, received the manifestations of esteem and affection which were showered upon him in later life.

What made Robert Jones a master surgeon ? He never would acknowledge that he possessed more than a most superficial acquaintance with physiology and the allied sciences ; indeed, he was not a man of high intellectual attainments, as usually estimated, yet, like H. O. Thomas, he had a most intimate practical understanding of the mechanics of support and the functions of movement, and an almost uncanny apprehension of the fourth dimension as applied to the physics of progression. But as to the fourth dimension itself, as explained, say, by Eddington, he would have smiled broadly and have disclaimed all understanding of it, without a hint that he was with the majority in this matter, although he would surely have suspected it.

He gained his wizardry by observation and a vast experience, allied to astounding powers of prognosis and to flawless surgical technique. One friend remembers how, in 1897, when fresh from the antiseptic training of King's College Hospital, he met Robert Jones at dinner and learnt from him of his aseptic management of operations on joints. A " draw " was declared by Robert Jones, in his sporting fashion, for he admitted to antiseptic preparation of the skin. How often since has that argument taken place.

William Mayo, in 1907, described Robert Jones's operative skill in the following words : " He is expeditious, yet neglects not the smallest detail, and his wonderful experience enables him to do wizard-like operations with a precision which is startling." So, too, with his manipulations of fractures and dislocations, he had the dexterity and the confidence of a conjurer.

Robert Jones's numerous contributions to his special branch of surgery were always clinical in character, and were based on the close study of unrivalled material. He certainly made many new observations, and these, as well as the principles of Thomas, which he fully endorsed and practised, have never been refuted by physiological and pathological advances made by others.

The first serious contribution to orthopædic surgery made by Robert Jones, who published alone or in collaboration four monographs and about sixty papers, concerned the method of reduction of Colles's fracture (" An Analysis of 105 Cases of Colles's Fracture," 1884). He then made temporary excursions into the purlieus of general surgery, in which no doubt he engaged in his early days, as his uncle had always done, and he communicated a paper on the method of treating hæmorrhoids by suture—a procedure often ascribed to Thelwall Thomas—and another on " Four Cases of Perforating Gastric Ulcer," upon which he had operated. Subsequent publications on the operative treatment of infantile spastic paralysis and of spondylitis announced his return to the orthopædic fold, from which he strayed no more. In the next fifteen years the same number of clinical contributions came from his pen.

In 1909 Robert Jones revealed his vast experience in his " Notes on Derangements of the Knee," illustrated by the records of 500 cases. This classical study set the seal on his growing fame.

Possibly in the years to come the constant insistence by Robert Jones of the *functional necessity of alignment, rather than mere end-to-end apposition, of fractured bones*, will stand out as his most original and scientific contribution to his art. Robert Jones was also the first surgeon successfully to transplant the flexor muscles of the forearm into the extensors in a case of irreparable injury to the musculospiral nerve. Moreover, his untiring advocacy of tendon transplantation, bone grafting, and other conservative and physiologically restorative procedures, has led to the general adoption of such methods, the beauty as well as the usefulness of which so greatly appealed to him.

There has been much discussion as to the part Robert Jones and Thurstan Holland played in introducing Röntgen's rays to surgical practice in this country. In a letter,

11 Nelson Street, Liverpool.
The house in which Hugh Owen Thomas and Robert Jones practised. Now occupied by Mr. T. P. McMurray, formerly the assistant of Robert Jones.

To face p. 184

Holland states: "Röntgen's discovery was made public in Germany late in December, 1895; I think the date was December 27th. A German lady who came to Robert Jones's free Sunday clinic to help on an early Sunday in January, 1896, insisted on reading to R. J. and myself a letter from a relation in Germany describing the discovery. We both laughed at her. We were probably the first in England to hear the news—at least a week, if not more, before any notice appeared in an English paper. In February, 1896, through R. J., I accompanied a youth to the laboratory of Oliver Lodge—the youth was supposed to have a small pistol-bullet in his hand . . . finally, a very hazy plate showed the shadow of the bullet. . . . Later, R. J., seeing that the discovery must be of use to him, asked me to order an apparatus at his expense and experiment with it. [Thurstan Holland at that time was in general practice, and was well known as a most expert amateur photographer.] In May, 1896, I took my first X-ray. R. J. was at the Southern Hospital then, and shortly afterwards (in the same year) this hospital bought an apparatus and appointed me as radiologist. That is the true and authentic account of our start in Liverpool."

Still, before a man can be considered a master surgeon, he must accomplish more than that which results from personal skill and acumen; he must establish and hand on something by which other men, perhaps less skilful and less able, can benefit the generations to follow; and this in no small measure is exactly what Robert Jones did. Moynihan once said at a dinner in honour of Robert Jones, that it is not only in what a man himself does, it is not only in the books that he writes, but it is in the disciples he leaves behind him, that his name will live. Although this is not of universal application, it was certainly true of his subject. Robert Jones was, it cannot be denied, the shepherd of orthopædics. He brought safely into the fold the wild and scattered lambs; he tended them; he controlled them; he improved their quality; and he so surely perpetuated the breed that the world in its hour of need was furnished from his stock.

The attributes which caused him, when his great opportunity came during the War, to be surrounded by eager disciples ready to obey his slightest behest, and afterwards to convey his principles to the furthermost parts of the earth, were manifold. His consummate knowledge of his subject and his power of conveying to all the principles on which his practice was based alone would hardly have succeeded to the extent that actually occurred; it was, besides, his personal attraction and power of drawing men into communion (rather than consultation) with him that secured willing co-operation. He made his youngest colleague feel that he, Robert Jones himself, was seeking for light in their discussions.

This relationship was based on his own modesty and ever-present generosity in regard to knowledge, which he always presumed to exist in others. In consequence, his clinics were of the nature of friendly displays in which he sank his own identity. All this made his epiphany the more effective. Robert Jones alone in action was a figure of amazing efficiency, be it as an organiser or as a surgeon.

A word must be said of Robert Jones as an expert witness. He was astonishing—unique. He would take the judge, jury, counsel and court into his confidence. It was quite impossible to cross-examine him, he was so patently honest and sincere. By common consent, he at once became a Court of Appeal in himself.

It cannot be denied that Fortune favoured him, and, indeed, she would have been a scurvy Fortune had she frowned on so gentle and so gallant a knight. She gave him his first great opportunity when he became apprenticed to Hugh Owen Thomas; and his second, while he was still a young man, on the Manchester Ship Canal; and, finally, she arranged that he should have reached just that age and eminence which prevented his being overlooked when the War came. He availed himself to the full of these opportunities for which he was so specially suited.

At the end of hostilities His Majesty the King, in conferring an honour, said to Robert Jones: "Your services have been invaluable to the State on behalf of my poor wounded. You have done splendid work. Thank you!" A great compliment, indeed, a tribute of affection, was also paid to him by that most generous Director-General of Army Medical Services, Sir John Goodwin.

Robert Jones had in very truth given inestimable service. He had, moreover, brought Thomas's splint into its own, and the lives and limbs of thousands of grateful men had been preserved through the instrumentality of this apparatus. In Liverpool he established a hospital with 600 beds for orthopædic cases alone, under the charge of his skilful assistant, T. P. McMurray; and about 100 of these beds were allotted to patients with war-fractured femora, among whom the mortality was trifling in comparison with that obtaining in previous wars, thanks to the immediate application in casualty clearing stations of Thomas's splint.

Space only permits mention in this connection of the network of orthopædic centres which he organised throughout the country, and the workshops associated with them which he established to lead wounded men usefully and happily from war to peace. In this he showed statesmanship of a very high order. His surgery and his orthopædic centres have paved the way for the proper treatment of civilian injuries in factories and elsewhere throughout the world.

Behind all this, and winding like fairy threads through his life work, were his efforts for the relief of crippledom. It was in the year 1898 that Robert Jones came to realise that the work he was doing for crippled children should be developed as a social service. From that year to the end of his life he devoted his time, his mind, and his skill to the organisation of facilities and the perfection of technique for this humanitarian crusade.

His alliance with Dame Agnes Hunt, his work in aid of the Country Hospitals for Children near Liverpool, and his attempts to stimulate the national conscience in this matter—the prevention and cure of crippled children—may, indeed, in the years to come serve even more than his orthopædic surgery during the War to establish his claim to immortality as one of the greatest and most thoughtful of the benefactors of humanity. It is delightful to know that in this great work his heart was no less concerned than his surgical vision, for he was a lover of children and a tower of strength to the weak.

Naturally, then, we are led to study Robert Jones as a man, and to inquire into his habits, characteristics and tastes, for, as already foreshadowed, from these we may obtain some guidance in our search for the factors responsible for his beneficent career.

Meeting Robert Jones in his late maturity, many may have been tempted to wonder whether his happy disposition, friendly cordiality, and modest demeanour were not the outcome of success, for success has a mellowing effect on some. If, however, they had known Robert Jones as a young man they would have recognised that he had always a boyish, springy, gay and courageous attitude towards life. One night he had been to visit a patient of his uncle in the Brownlow Street area, then a slum region. "Dancing along," as he was wont to relate, for he never walked in those days when he could run, he came across a big, drunken navvy thrashing his wife in the street. " As I passed him," he would say, " I let fly and caught him on the point. He fell with a crash to the pavement, and I took to my heels and raced for home. All that night I lay in bed shivering with fear. I realised that he might have fractured his skull, and that I might be arrested for manslaughter." Luckily the man's skull was too thick to be fractured by a fall on the pavement, but Robert Jones avoided the street for many days. His boxing proclivities, it may be mentioned, caused him concern on another occasion, when he put the professional whom he paid to box with him in Nelson Street soundly " to sleep," and spent an anxious time reviving him.

It will be seen that Robert Jones was a sportsman : he saw every important fight he could. He never quite forgave Beckett for being knocked out by Carpentier while he was putting his hat under his seat. His interest in cricket was no less. During the twenty-four hours, which elapsed between the first and fatal heart attack which led to his death, he asked his daughter to switch on the wireless that he might hear how a test match in Australia was progressing. He was, too, a keen and at one time a fine game shot ; indeed, within a few days of his death he was shooting ; but he realised then that such activities were getting beyond his powers. Despite this, he had a horror of giving in, and to the last he refused to realise how ill he was.

It may well be that too much attention is paid to sport of all kinds in the world to-day ; but there can be no doubt that to the professional man a love of sport and engagement in it provide the necessary means for concentration in another direction. If he cannot keep his eye on the ball, he probably has his mind on some obscure case.

Besides, sport has a class-levelling influence and gives a man an insight into the mentality of a variety of specimens of humanity. Robert Jones was at home, and could converse in their own language, with the professional boxers, footballers and cricketers who so often sought his aid, no less than with the little maiden whose doll had a fractured leg which he gravely "set," and with the Royal lady whose thigh he absent-mindedly slapped, to the horror of her medical attendant, as he emphasised the points concerned in the treatment of the damaged knee which was slung over his own leg.

His interest in literature and art was considerable, and one met in his house the greatest authors and actors of the day. He was, too, a lover of oratory; he had listened to Bright, to Spurgeon, and to Gladstone.

No doubt his freedom from ill-health, except occasional attacks of gout, until towards the end of his days, and his active extrospective life, combined with his extraordinary unselfishness and interest in the doings of others and his power of seeing himself as a figure of fun, were responsible for his delightful and infectious happiness. That he had succeeded unaided in tying the laces of his shoes, when a certain portliness rendered this somewhat difficult, would be celebrated by the merry humming of a pæan of victory—a little thing, but pregnant with meaning.

His generosity knew no bounds, and his friends soon learned that to praise his wine or to admire a possession was a certain way of giving a licence to his love of bestowing gifts.

Those privileged to enjoy his affection will always remember the evenings spent dining with him *tête-à-tête*, and the animated discussions which followed. For them, an imperishable memory is that of Robert Jones sitting in his easy-chair with his elbows on the arms and his spread finger-tips rapidly impinging on each other, while he quickly crossed and recrossed his extended feet in accompaniment with a rapid flow of words.

There was in him a childlike confidence in his friends, indeed, in the world at large. He accepted everyone at his face value, and it was unthinkable that anyone should deceive him. Nevertheless, his gaiety and happiness became sadly overcast when he thought someone whom he knew was not playing the game. It is a mistake, however, to suppose that he was happy-go-lucky in his estimates of men and their methods. He was not ; he was singularly acute, and he could, when he thought the occasion demanded, express his opinion quite definitely, forcibly and finally. Robert Jones, no different in this respect from other men, had predilections, preferences and prejudices ; but these he kept to himself. Needless to say, there was always a just reason for his views ; but he had an absolute horror of hurting anyone's feelings. There was one blemish in character, however, namely, pose, which gave him intense amusement, and about which he did not hesitate to speak, for he had an excellent repertory of stories. He himself was the most natural man in the world, his self-effacement was almost a vice, and he could neither understand nor appreciate the necessity for pose in lesser beings. He recognised that pose is a cloak for inferiority ; and that the cloak often takes the form of assumed superiority.

Ceremonial functions did not appeal to him, public speaking he disliked, and if it were possible to put on his military accoutrements and his orders wrongly, assuredly he did so. At one function several ladies went on their knees to salve his breast-load of decorations which at an awkward moment clattered to the floor. That he should have been taken behind a bush at Buckingham Palace to have his uniform properly arranged, was no unusual incident. Robert Jones was, as we have seen, intensely human, and his best stories were those he told of his own (often assumed) discomfiture on such occasions.

It seemed almost impossible that so vital, so buoyant a personality—one who was so active and happy in his work—could suddenly become enfeebled, while still daily insisting on his well-being, and in the course of a few months pass from the world in which he has left such fragrant remembrances, such dazzling memories, and so enduring a name.

The last public function he attended was the opening by the Duchess of York of the House of the British College of Obstetricians and Gynæcologists, on December 5th, 1932, when he received an Honorary Fellowship. This was the last of the very large number of academic distinctions which had been conferred upon him by British and foreign colleges and universities, and which removed all doubts as to the justice of his official rewards.

A grey day in January, 1933. The walls of his home, no longer hospitable, appeared unchanged ; but no laughter echoed from them. Within the house seemed empty, yet the furniture was untouched, and the library was full of well-known faces which looked as though a chilling wind had been frozen into them. Colleagues, friends, relatives, servants stood silent, each desolate, remote and bereft ; the spirit had gone out of the place. Gone was the friendly, happy, embracing warmth of his welcome which all knew so well, and on which they pondered while waiting to be taken to the resting place where the ashes of Robert Jones were to lie for all time on an altar illumined by shafts of light through the window. Service, in the Protestant

Cathedral of Liverpool. Here, in the sight of a vast gathering, a last tribute was paid to the man who had been taken from us. His noble example and his far-seeing work for humanity remain for all time.

W. B.-B.

XXI PATRICK MANSON

(1844–1922)

TROPICAL MEDICINE

THE time has now arrived when it is possible to envisage the career of this great Scotsman as a whole, and to assess the position which his work is destined to hold in the realm of science. The life of Manson may well be regarded as an epoch, for he initiated a new era in medicine, viz., the association of the spread of disease in man with the agency of winged insects. This was such a revolutionary conception that it could only be gradually accepted by the majority of the medical profession, and still more gradually by the lay public. It may be argued that there were others before the subject of this biography who had in some hazy way associated certain diseases with the presence of insect life, but there it remained more as a nebulous idea than as a concrete and proven fact. Manson did more than this : he infused a new spirit of adventure into British Colonial administration, and with this he embodied a new spirit of hope for the colonisation of those parts of the tropics which had been conquered by British initiative, and he started and fathered the teaching of a new department of medicine—Tropical Medicine—of which he is now justly regarded as the greatest master of all time.

Manson was born on October 3rd, 1844, in a small but ancient village in Aberdeenshire. He came of a humble but, nevertheless, sturdy lineage, and his ancestors hailed from the land of the Vikings. The name of Manson is

SIR PATRICK MANSON, G.C.M.G., M.D., F.R.S.
1844–1922

To face p. 194

still a common surname in the Orkney and Shetland Islands.

Debarred by some physical defect from following the career of an engineer, on which his heart was at first set, he entered the lists of medicine at the age of sixteen, with no doubts about his future success, for at the age of twenty-one we find him fully qualified and equipped for the fight of life, and, moreover, earning his own living. Before he was twenty-two he had emigrated to Formosa and had made his first acquaintance with the medical mysteries of the East. Compared with the modern youth, what preparation had he enjoyed to fit him for a career of scientific exploration? The more we ponder upon it, the more we are struck with amazement that this modest Scotsman with such poor preparation was enabled for this next fifty years of his life to make one discovery of first-class importance after another, and to add so many new and original methods of laboratory research, as well as technical improvements in surgery, ophthalmology and medicine.

Manson spent some five years in the wilds of Formosa, but during that period he appears to have acted in the rôle of student and observer, and in 1870 he moved to the mainland, to Amoy, the Treaty port in the Bay of Hiu Tau. There he spent another five years before his mind turned seriously towards his life work.

Returning to England in 1875, having amassed a store of practical knowledge in all the branches of practical medicine and surgery in which he had been entirely self-taught, he found in the dusty precincts of the reading room of the British Museum the spark that kindled the flaming torch; for there he stumbled across the writings of one Timothy Lewis, an officer in the Army Medical Service in India, and an original mind of the first calibre. This Lewis had found in Calcutta a minute worm in the blood of the natives he had examined in that city, but beyond noting it as a curiosity, no particular significance had been attached to this discovery. With that far-seeing insight which afterwards became the chief characteristic in Manson's scientific make-up, he foresaw the connection between this—the *Filaria sanguinis hominis* (the filaria of human blood)—a thread-like connection with that most disfiguring disease, elephantiasis, which had been such a familiar sight to him in the streets of Amoy. In London and in Edinburgh he familiarised himself with the technique of the compound microscope, which had then been introduced as an aid to medical practice, and procuring the best possible, and also having married the charming lady who is now Lady Manson, he returned to his post at the close of 1875. From that time onwards there issued a stream of papers which were printed in the non-medical pages of the reports of the Imperial Maritime Customs Service of China. This work, as it may be called, contained at that time the writings of many distinguished men dealing with many aspects of life in China; it embodied a wealth of information hardly to be found in any similar publication of that kind, and it affords at the present day some kind of an index to the sort of work these British pioneers did for the Chinese Empire. It was to this fortuitous fact that Manson's many medical writings came to be so tardily appreciated by the medical profession as a whole. His first papers upon the *Filaria sanguinis hominis* amongst the Chinese and the wonderful and still unexplained fact of its periodic appearance in the blood stream during the hours of the night, attracted the notice of the greatest helminthologist of the time—Thomas Cobbold—who wrote appreciatively of the work and ideas of what he considered to be a rather eccentric Scotsman, in the pages of *The Lancet* and of *The Veterinarian*. But when this startling account of the vagaries of a minute worm in the human body which appeared to possess the uncanny knowledge of the exact time of the day and night, was capped by the statement that in order to pass from the body of one man to another, the services of a winged insect or mosquito was necessary to act as a nurse, there was great astonishment. The paper, which embodies this work, appeared in the *Transactions of the Linnean Society of London* in 1879, and its presentation by Cobbold gave rise to a prolonged and not very discerning discussion ; in fact it was regarded as the vapourings of an ill-equipped dreamer who worked in a far-off country of which only a few persons had ever heard.

It was in August, 1877, that Manson persuaded his Chinese servant—Huito by name—to make himself a living sacrifice on the altar by allowing himself to sleep in a mosquito cage where he could be freely bitten at night-time by the brown mosquito of Amoy, which we now recognise as *Culex fatigans*. Manson had known for some time that this servant harboured in his blood many of these minute filariæ, and that they periodically emerged from the interior of his body in large numbers at night, so the next morning he collected the engorged and fed female insects in large numbers in separate bottles, and endeavoured to keep them alive as long as was possible. Owing to the defective knowledge of the life habits of the mosquito at this time, he was unable to do so for a longer period than five days, but during this time he made numerous dissections of the body tissues of the mosquitoes, which he killed by administering a puff of tobacco smoke. The instruments he used for dissection, too, were primitive, and consisted of fine pen-nibs. He was not long in discovering that, much to his astonishment, the minute worms had migrated from where they were entangled in the blood in the mosquito's stomach into the tissues of the thorax, and he was able to ascertain that they were undergoing a remarkable change in shape and size, and he realised—as he put it in his own words—that he had "stumbled upon an important fact with a distinct bearing upon human pathology," and he followed it up as best he could with the meagre appliances at his disposal. After many months of work, often following up false trails, he ultimately succeeded in tracing the filaria into the thoracic muscles of the mosquito, where it was manifestly on its road to a new human host.

Few books on entomology had then been written, and the knowledge of the anatomy of insect life was meagre in the extreme. Manson endeavoured to learn all he could by his own personal observations on the anatomy of the mosquito, and after much solicitation he obtained from the British Museum the only extant work in this realm of zoology, which turned out to be a treatise on the anatomy of the cockroach.

Although Manson received at all times much valuable help and encouragement from fellow practitioners in that far-off portion of the world, yet there was no one to whom he could turn for scientific advice or help, and thus we find him writing to Cobbold: "Men, like myself, in general practice, are but poor and slow investigators, crippled as we are with the necessity of making our daily bread."

Some few people have left us an impression of Manson at that time, and it was that of a handsome, upstanding, athletic and healthy man, immersed in the activities of life, with practical medicine, surgery, with the pleasures of outdoor life, hunting, fishing and shooting, looking far more like a country squire than one engaged in the elucidation of the major problems of scientific medicine. There never was anything of the haggard, pale-faced and bespectacled student, the type of a popular conception, in Manson's personality.

One of the great difficulties of his work in China was to obtain autopsies on the human body in order to find out the exact pathology of elephantiasis, leprosy and many other interesting diseases. Twice only during his career in China, at the imminent risk of his life, and only by entering native cemeteries at the dead of night by the light of a lantern, did he succeed in performing this necessary office. Once he was disappointed after bargaining with the patient himself and his prospective widow to buy his body for one hundred dollars, only to find himself eventually chased down the streets by an infuriated mob. But whenever he did obtain an autopsy he discovered a helminth new to science, and which he was able to describe and to name. So, failing with human material, he had recourse to animals, the dissection of dogs, cats and birds, notably the Chinese magpie and the crow, in whose blood he found filaria worms resembling those of the human beings. But even here he found his way blocked by the inexplicable Chinese traditions which forbade him to shoot any more of these birds, because the magpie is a sacred bird in China, as it harbours the soul of a Chinese Emperor who died many hundreds of years ago.

It was about this time that a lucky chance presented him with the discovery of an entirely new human parasite, and, as had happened before, it came to him in a peculiarly unrehearsed manner. One day a very self-possessed and important Chinese Mandarin entered his consulting room, and very insultingly spat on the floor at Manson's feet, ignoring completely the numerous sawdust-filled cuspidors which were arranged around the walls. Although blushing with indignation, Manson's scientific enthusiasm was satisfied by seeing that the sputum was tinged and streaked with blood, so seizing some with the forceps which he held in his hand, and placing it under the microscope, he discovered the eggs of a hitherto unknown worm, which turned out to be those of the lung fluke *Paragonimus* ; so that instead of kicking the insulting Chinaman out of his consulting room, as he first intended to do, he finished up by warmly congratulating him and shaking him by the hand. Then collecting some more of this sputum, he placed it in a glass bottle upon his desk, and added some tap water. In the rush of other work, he forgot all about making further observations on the eggs, until one day some six weeks afterwards, noticing an offensive smell that emanated from this particular bottle, he bethought himself of examining the sediment still further under the microscope before throwing it away. Once again by the most fortunate chance, he observed the small ciliated embryo, or *miracidium*, trying to force its way out of the egg, and manifestly also on its way to a new host. Thus was initiated the first steps of the wonderful life history of this fluke as it is understood at the present day.

In 1883 Manson emigrated with his family to Hongkong, and there in the next period of seven years he was responsible for initiating a new era in the medical life of that city. With his vast accumulated store of medical knowledge, and backed up by a brilliant reputation which had spread throughout the whole of China, it was not long before he amassed an enormous general practice. About this time he began to suffer severely from periodic attacks of gout, which remained his chief enemy throughout the rest of his long life. In spite of frequent crippling attacks, he was engaged at full speed for nearly every minute of the twenty-four hours, and the practice which he formed at this time has now descended to a firm of European doctors in that city.

One day a very excitable American naturalist who had been hunting birds in the wilds of Formosa, rushed into his

View of Amoy, 1873, showing Manson's house on the summit of the hill beneath the arrow.

Manson in retirement, trout fishing on Lough Mask, Co. Galway, 1919.

consulting room with streams of blood pouring from his nose. He thought his end had come, but Manson, after inquiring what part of the jungle he had worked in, and after an appreciative grunt, produced a nasal speculum and a syringeful of salt water, and looking up his nostril, perceived a large leech tucked away in the upper nares. After injecting the salt water, he removed it with a pair of forceps, and it fell into a basin in front of the astonished gaze of the victim, who, seized by terror, dashed out of the room with his handkerchief to his nose, calling upon his God, and was never seen again. His chief contributions to science at this time were centred mainly in attempts to find the parasite which caused malaria, as he was entirely ignorant of the discovery which had been made by Laveran in 1880.

It was for his organisation of medical studies that his public work in Hongkong will be most remembered. He was the founder of the Medical Society of Hongkong; he was the founder and first president of the Medical School of Hongkong which attempted to impart medical knowledge to Chinese students and which has since blossomed out as the University of Hongkong of the present day. He found time, moreover, to found and organise a dairy in order to provide the necessary cows' milk for the sick and needy children of the European community and for the soldiers of the garrison. Amongst other medical subjects of general interest we may note that at this time he described accurately the disease which we now know as sprue, and was the first to insist upon the necessity of its treatment by milk and liver soup. Manson obtained his knowledge of the value of liver in the treatment of this disease from the Chinese native doctors themselves, and he remained a constant advocate of the therapeutic value of liver treatment.

At the end of 1889 Manson returned to Scotland, where he had acquired an estate in the vicinity of his birthplace, and where he intended to pass the remainder of his days as a man of leisure ; but luckily for posterity, fate had it otherwise. The large fortune that he had accumulated rapidly diminished in the face of the falling value of the Chinese dollar, so that in the ensuing year he was forced to begin work again, and descending upon London, he commenced a consulting practice at 21 Queen Anne Street. Although his reputation had been unequalled in the East, he found that it was not so easy to commence an uphill struggle at forty-six years of age ; but soon his connection began, and it was not long before he was appointed a physician to the Seamen's Hospital Society, with charge of beds in the Dreadnought Hospital at Greenwich. There he found a mass of unutilised clinical material of great interest. He soon discovered that beri-beri was prevalent amongst the seamen who flocked to the Port of London from the tropical ports, furthermore he was able to confirm and extend the recent discoveries upon the malaria parasite, and at the same time to give demonstrations upon these diseases. By good fortune, too, there were many cases of guineaworm infection at his disposal, and on these he was able to demonstrate the remarkable life-history of this parasite in a practical way, and was able to trace its development in the body cavity of a species of cyclops which he captured in the pond at Hampstead Heath. Furthermore, by obtaining specimens of blood from patients from Central Africa, and soliciting friends to send him blood slides from all parts of the world, he was able in a short time to describe as new to science three new species of blood filaria.

In a small room at the top of his house, which was euphoniously dubbed " the muck room," he conducted many experiments on mice, rats and birds, and there he bred artificially various species of mosquito ; in fact, this room soon became the meeting ground of all those in London who were interested in the development of this new branch, which became known as Tropical Medicine. Some years were spent in an enquiry into the curious phenomenon known as the exflagellation of the malaria parasite. Up to this time it had been regarded as representing the death agony of the parasite before it finally perished in the blood stream. Manson thought otherwise, for he regarded it as the first stage of its life story, and as meaning that in nature this process had to be gone through in the body cavity of some winged insect. And thus it came about that in 1894, on his first meeting with the young enthusiast from India—Ronald Ross—he was able to explain to him what he gave out as the *mosquito-malaria* hypothesis ; and as is well known, the period of the next five years, from 1894–9, was spent mainly in encouraging and advising Ross, who was then in India, on this historic quest. About 1897, Manson commenced a series of lectures with the idea of stimulating the Government of the day to provide special instruction in tropical medicine with the object of preventing, as far as possible, the terrible mortality which was disgracing the annals of British Colonial administration. In this he found a firm and great coadjutor in the person of Joseph Chamberlain, then, as now, the greatest Colonial Secretary that Great Britain has ever possessed. The year 1899 was the opening of the London School of Tropical Medicine at the Albert Dock, where Manson taught almost daily, where he came to be regarded as the one and only oracle, and as the guide, philosopher and friend of every student that entered its portals. How this school has flourished, and how it has become transformed into the important and imposing structure known as the London School of Hygiene and Tropical Medicine at the present day, is a story familiar to all, and to Manson it remained almost his chief object and care until his retirement in 1913.

From 1897 to 1913 he acted as adviser and consultant to the Colonial Office, and his hand is to be seen in almost every step of major importance in the Colonial Medical Administration of that period. He was responsible for the creation of the West African Medical Service; he was responsible for the establishment of research institutions in the chief Colonies, in Tropical Africa and in Malaya; and, moreover, he was responsible for the proper presentation of medical reports and the collection of scientific data in the Colonial Medical Services all over the world.

During his nine years of retirement before his death on April 9th, 1922, Manson spent a great deal of his time in the wilds of Western Ireland in County Galway, engaged in his particular pastime of fishing: for, like many of his distinguished predecessors, Manson was a devoted follower of Izaak Walton.

It is good to think that there are many memorials in existence to the work of this great man. It is good to think that as time goes on his name and fame, so far from becoming obscured by the mists of time, are flashing forth with a still stronger and steadier light. In recollections of the great men of the past, and in addresses given by the leaders of our profession at the present day, we see the name of Manson frequently mentioned in the same breath as that of the great heroes of our science, those of Pasteur, Lister and Koch. There are memorials of his name in Manson House, now the head-quarters of the Royal Society of Tropical Medicine in Portland Place. The writer has the honour of serving in two Manson wards, the one at the Royal Albert Dock Hospital, where clinical tropical medicine first saw the light of day, and the other at the Hospital for Tropical Diseases. There is a Manson Clinical

Theatre for the instruction of students in tropical medicine at this hospital as well, and the Museum of the present School of Hygiene and Tropical Medicine is called after him. In the Hall of this building is a very fine bronze plaque executed by the French sculptor, P. Richer, and which was the original of the memento presented to him at the International Congress of Medicine which met in London in 1913.

Like all truly great men, Manson was a simple, honest man ; these very qualities shone from his face and were evidenced in every action that he undertook. He was, moreover, kindly, courteous and tolerant, and of a disposition which was equally beloved by his patients and by his colleagues. In his scientific mental make-up he appeared to be always guided by the rules of nature, and he was by his upbringing a careful and accurate observer of all living things around him : a great gardener, a good sportsman and a good fisherman, so that he viewed all human problems in the same broad and magnanimous spirit with which he tended the roses in his garden. Gifted with great powers of imagination and foresight, he was able to envisage to himself the probable course of disease, and it was this essential sanity of his which made him the great prophet of tropical medicine.

Some object to the title of " The Father of Tropical Medicine " which has been applied to him on many occasions, but it is difficult not to acknowledge this claim when it is remembered that what was so obscure before his time has now all become as clear as the light of day, and the main solution of these problems has been due to the fact that the majority of Manson's hypotheses have become true.

It is rare to find a man of science of this nature who combines with it a general sagacity of the affairs of men, and is an organiser of the first rank ; but such a man was

Manson, and all that he has built has been set upon such secure foundations that it is no exaggeration to foretell that his work, and that all he founded in the space of his fifty years of active life, will remain secure for ever.

P. H. M.-B.

SIR WILLIAM OSLER, Bt.
1849–1919

To face p. 207

XXII WILLIAM OSLER
(1849–1919)

HUMANITIES AND MEDICINE

WHEN an American speaks of Sir William Osler one usually hears undiluted eulogy ; and if attention is called to this fact, the reply is almost inevitable : " How could it be anything else ? " The effect of his work and of his personality extends throughout the entire compass of the United States. Anecdotes pour in about him, and they grow. Many medical schools and libraries have been enriched through him, and the seed he sowed is multiplying. Wherever he went the study of medical history was sure to develop.

Osler was of Anglo-Saxon and Celtic stock, which was adventurous and vigorous with marked initiative. His father, a Canon of the Church of England, migrated with his wife to take a charge on the borders of the Canadian wilderness, lured, we believe, largely by the dangers and hardships involved, for both of which Canon Osler and his young bride seemed to have a natural urge. William was their eighth child and third son. He was born at Bond Head, Ontario, in 1849. On the death of an elder brother in 1901, a Canadian paper referred to the family as one that had produced more distinguished men than any other contemporary family in the Commonwealth.

On Sir William's seventieth birthday, when Regius Professor of Physic at Oxford, with tributes showered upon him from all parts of the world, he gave this running outline of his life: "Toronto, Montreal, London, Berlin, Vienna, as a student; Montreal, Philadelphia, Baltimore, Oxford, as a teacher—many cities, many men. Truly, with Ulysses, I may say, 'I am a part of all that I have met.'" He was; and all who met him felt the bond. He saw everything and everybody from the inside. Nevertheless, paradoxically, he was, as he once said, "British to the core." His love for England was a son's love; for the world at large he held a brother's warm affection.

Osler's medical achievements are often underestimated by those who knew him and had become obsessed by the charm of his personality. But under that charm was the substance. A scholar, a skilled pathologist, a great clinician, a humanist—he was all of these. His love for his profession was little short of idolatry. That a man should make of it a business was to him anathema. Let his words in his address, "Teacher and Student," speak for him: "My message is chiefly to you, students of medicine, since with the ideals entertained now your future is indissolubly bound. The choice lies open, the paths are plain before you. Always seek your own interests, make of a high and sacred calling a sordid business, regard your fellow creatures as so many tools of trade, and if your heart's desire is for riches, they may be yours; but you will have bartered away the birthright of a noble heritage, traduced the physician's well-deserved title of the 'Friend of Man,' and falsified the best traditions of an ancient and honourable guild."

After the days of his mischievous boyhood until his death, work and humanity were the master words of his life; his purpose was to unite the art and science of medicine. It would be difficult, even in a lengthy biography, to keep pace with his activities. He gave the effect, so rarely seen in human beings, and always seen in nature, of the radiance of an apparently effortless energy.

> " Who has seen the wind ?
> Neither you nor I,
> Yet when the trees bow down their heads
> The wind is passing by."

So it was with William Osler in his passage through the world.

It seems to be accorded that the high watermark of his medical productiveness was the sixteen years spent at the Johns Hopkins in Baltimore, 1889–1905. " Here," writes William H. Welch, " he made his two greatest contributions to medicine, the most important being the creation of the first medical clinic worthy of the name in any English-speaking country, and the other the publication, in 1892, of his text-book, presenting with literary skill and unexampled success the principles and practice of medicine, adequately and completely, for the first time in English after the great revolutionary changes brought about by modern bacteriology."

Osler's ambition was expressed in a farewell address in America in 1905 : " To make myself a good clinical physician . . . to build a great clinic on Teutonic lines, not on those previously followed here and in England, but on lines that have placed the scientific medicine of Germany in the forefront of the world. And if I have done anything to promote the growth of clinical medicine, it has been in this direction in the formation of a large clinic with a well-organised series of assistants and house physicians, and with proper laboratories in which to work at the intricate problems that confront us in internal medicine." Dr. Welch points out that in America, " Osler improved upon the German model by engrafting upon it the English system of clinical clerkships."

To human beings Osler's attitude, always overkindly, varied in a marked degree. To his colleagues he was the good comrade; to his students, the Socratic teacher, the "young man's friend"; and when a pupil of his went out into the world to fend for himself, Osler was his unvarying advocate. With children, with whom he was happiest, he was just a child himself, and his boyish love of farce was a source of delight to them and to his students. Now and then his contemporaries and elders failed to be amused, but very rarely; he somehow managed to refresh the atmosphere with everything he did—even with his practical jokes. But it was at the bedside of the sick poor that one had a glimpse into the heart of William Osler in its beautiful compassion.

In 1892, when forty-two years of age, he married Grace Revere Gross, the widow of a former colleague, Samuel Gross, a distinguished surgeon of Philadelphia. The marriage was a superlatively fortunate one. It enabled Osler to give his entire time to his profession without the handicap of small worries, and it made for him a home which his students and colleagues found was also theirs. To call his welcome hospitality seems a misnomer, it was so spontaneous, so apparently free from any forethought or care on the part of host or hostess. It was their pleasure, not their duty. Dr. and Mrs. Osler had two sons: one died shortly after birth, and the other, Edward Revere Osler, was mortally wounded on the Ypres salient on August 29th, 1917, in his twenty-first year.

The rapidity with which Osler worked, his power to concentrate at a glance upon the essentials, made him effective in every direction; and not a moment of his time was unoccupied. Though he was grievously overburdened, it was impossible for any one to recognise this, so deceptive was the inspiring vitality of his manner. But when, in 1905, he was called to the Regius Professorship of Physic at Oxford, in spite of the pang of regret at curtailing his clinical work and losing his intimate relations with his students, he went to England as a man, after a long journey, goes home. According to his habit, he instantly became again a part of the life about him. Sir Clifford Albutt, in his preface to the " Memorial Volume " presented to Sir William on the seventieth anniversary of his birthday, best expresses his adaptability and unifying power : " Thus, almost with the rapidity of thought, between Canada, the United States and Great Britain an academic link three-fold was forged. In no person as well as in your own could this unity have been so happily consummated ; you arrived, indeed, from overseas, but as a pilgrim child of Oxford. In you the literary and historical traditions of the beautiful city were united with the zeal and adventure of the New World."

The last years of Sir William's life, from 1905 to 1919, were spent in England ; and if they were less productive in medical achievement they were somewhat like the mellowing of a rare vintage wine, deepening in quality and flavour. Until the coming of the War they were unquestionably the happiest years of a supremely fortunate existence. It was at Oxford that his avocation, the collecting of old medical writings and incunabula, had its full scope.

It is impossible in so short a sketch to do more than indicate a few of Sir William's beneficent activities in England. He entered into every phase of British medical life and increased its value. Sir Humphry Rolleston, in his Foreword to " Sir William Osler in Great Britain " (Memorial Volume, edited by Dr. Maude Abbott), speaks of Osler's "soon becoming the real though unobtrusive motive power in British medicine." One sees him a student of Christ Church; a Curator of the Bodleian Library; a Delegate to the University Press; Master of the old Alms House at Ewelme; President of the Bibliographical Society; and later President of the Classical Association, the first physician ever given this honour. Among the few honours that gave him pleasure and no work was the conferring upon him of a baronetcy at the time of the coronation of George V, in 1911.

When the War came Sir William devoted his every effort to do what he felt ought to be done; but he loathed war, and when his adored boy was killed, all who knew Sir William realised that, though he continued to work and to do for others, even whistling as he went, his heart was broken. An attack of pneumonia ended his life on December 29th, 1919.

Osler's contemporaries in the profession placed him among the great physicians of all ages. Sir George Newman, in his "Interpreters of Nature," expresses the universal feeling at the time of his death: "I have a sacred grove for my medical heroes, a sort of spiritual Valhalla, and there you will find Pasteur, Lister, Paget, Hutchinson; and there must now go the youthful-hearted, gay and charming Osler."

When not one shall be left who has felt the glamour of his presence, some feel that he will be best remembered by the priceless medical library he collected and bequeathed to McGill University, where his ashes are now preserved. Others believe that Sargent in his portrait of the Three Doctors which hangs in the Welch Memorial Library at Baltimore has caught his spirit and will hold it permanently before coming generations; others that his biographer, Dr. Harvey Cushing, has insured his immortality. And still others, of whom the writer is one, believe that, should medicine return to its birthright as the highest of all sacred professions, Osler, the great humanitarian physician, will be recognised as chief among its high priests.

E. G. R.

XXIII JAMES MACKENZIE

(1853–1924)

CARDIOLOGY

JAMES MACKENZIE was born in 1853 at Scone. The son of a farmer, he first attended the local school, and later on the Academy at Perth. When fifteen years of age he left school. Up till this time he did not distinguish himself particularly as a scholar. The routine of school training with the usual insistence on the assimilation of facts and learning by rote seems to have had but little effect on his already searching original mind. Then came the decision to become an apprentice to a dispensing chemist. At the age of twenty-one he went to Edinburgh to study medicine. During his years as chemist's apprentice must have been sown the seeds of the determination to go further and become a medical practitioner. Starting at Edinburgh, he was a good deal older than the majority of his associates. But here at the University the system of education was not easy for him. Just as at school, the importance of mere memory knowledge made it hard for his reasoning mind to assimilate facts. He had difficulty in passing his examinations. The system of education did little for his type of mind, to which the stages of logical deduction came easy, but the amassing of ill-digested knowledge and unrelated facts, hard.

After a period as a resident in the Edinburgh Royal Infirmary, Mackenzie went as assistant to Dr. Henry Briggs and Dr. John Brown, in Burnley, in the year 1879. As so

JAMES MACKENZIE
1853–1924

To face p. 214

often happens, Mackenzie had not been long in practice before he found that the knowledge of disease that he had acquired in his hospital training did not carry him very far in understanding the complaints for which his patients consulted him. How often does one hear the young general practitioner complain that he has to start learning quite a different sort of medicine from that which he thinks he has begun to master. That there is truth in this no one will deny; but, as Mackenzie made clear, the important thing is to go on learning. He was impressed with the great clinical sense and acumen which his partners possessed from long years of experience, but he felt to the full his disability in this direction. Faced, as general practitioners are, with the early vague manifestations of disease, his mind was constantly occupied with the prospects and prognosis of his cases. Books would not give him the information. He began to search and seek for himself. He realised that by watching and waiting certain results of disease would sooner or later certainly come to light. The meaning of the vague early symptoms, often without any physical signs, would be revealed. About the year 1883, he says: "I set myself the task of finding out the nature of the symptoms and signs I met with in the course of my practice. I had thus placed before me two definite objects at which to aim—(1) the understanding of the mechanism of symptoms, and (2) understanding of their prognostic significance." What a huge task he set himself to carry out single-handed. One can hardly admire enough the courage and resolution needed to tackle this immense problem. With this aim in view he set himself to make full notes of each and every symptom of which his patients complained. But he soon recognised the vast nature of this task, and restricted his observations to certain symptoms only.

The death of one of his patients from heart failure in

childbirth directed his attention particularly to disorders of the circulation. One of the first things to arouse his curiosity was irregularity of the pulse.

At this time any form of arrhythmia was apt to be looked upon as serious. No knowledge was available to distinguish between those that were of grave significance and those that were of trivial importance. So far no successful attempt had been made to unravel their meaning by graphic methods. There was, however, available the Dudgeon sphygmograph, and Mackenzie made use of this. Before long he had soon collected a large number of tracings, and it was apparent that a variety of arrhythmias existed. The difficulty was how to distinguish between them and how to assess their significance from the point of view of prognosis. The secret was not to be revealed by the sphygmograph alone. He next set himself to record the pulsation of the neck veins. At first the method was primitive—he gummed on pieces of straw. This method was soon improved by making use of a tambour similar to that which had been invented by Marey, but unknown to Mackenzie. The problem now was to correlate the jugular tracings with those obtained from the apex beat. A somewhat cumbersome apparatus was evolved, but the tracings were obtained. More difficult was the riddle of their interpretation.

It soon became clear that the second of the three jugular waves coincided with that of the apex beat. That the first wave was auricular naturally followed. But it was necessary to make a portable instrument and this was satisfactorily evolved. Unknown to Mackenzie, Potain and Reigel had already taken jugular tracings. But the exploitation of the knowledge to be gained by them all was left for him. As he said: "I attempted to *apply* this new knowledge in practice in various ways."

The first important fruit was soon ripe for picking. The

tracings showed that what is now the commonplace of medicine—the extra-systole—might be due to a premature beat of the ventricles. This discovery was viewed with a good deal of scepticism. But Mackenzie knew that he was on the right lines.

But he was not content alone with the elucidation of this form of arrhythmia. At the same time the significance had to be ascertained. So along with the search for the meaning of these signs was also carried on the interpretation of their importance. His records, now extending back some time, showed that where extra-systoles were the sole abnormality, their significance was small. Two points call for comment : This fundamentally new and revolutionary work was actually carried out in spite of all the calls of a busy general practice. A busy general practitioner had the courage and originality to put forward successfully these new and revolutionary ideas. The mere unravelling of the nature and significance of extra-systolic irregularities alone would be a life work for many men.

Along with this work he was observing the occurrence of sinus arrhythmia, " youthful irregularity " as he called it, as opposed to the " adult irregularity." Here, again, he was able to throw light on a dark ignorance that had caused many bogies to arise, and put fear into many hearts.

It did not escape him that one form of arrhythmia was associated with heart failure in many instances. He noted that the auricular wave was absent in the jugular tracings in these cases. But for some years the nature of the disturbance was obscure, until he had the long-waited opportunity to observe the onset of the trouble. Fortunately this occurred in a patient with mitral stenosis. Mackenzie did not fail to note the disappearance of the pre-systolic murmur. Linking this up with the absent auricular wave, and finding at autopsy that the patient's auricles were much dilated, he soon arrived at the fundamentally important conclusion that the auricles had ceased to beat. He called this condition paralysis of the auricles. These important discoveries were made during the nineties of the last century.

During this time the question of heart failure exercised his mind. The theory of " back pressure " due to valvular defects held the field. Mackenzie noted that the signs of congestive failure might coincide with the appearances of auricular fibrillation. But he soon saw that this was by no means a constant association. His keen mind soon perceived that the important cause of the failure was the tachycardia which the fibrillation was likely to produce. On this foundation were built two further important discoveries. In the first place he was able to put on a firm footing the rational use of digitalis to control the tachycardia and thereby relieve the congestive failure. Although Withering had written full enough directions in 1785 as to the use of this drug, during the last century much of its value had been wasted. Large enough doses were not given. We owe to Mackenzie the revival of rational digitalis therapy. In itself a large enough boon to mankind.

Then, as well, the question of heart failure had to be fitted into his observations. And following on his usual common-sense lines he was able to clear away the obscurities of the past, and enumerate perhaps the most important of all his ideas, that the health and efficiency of the myocardium is really the only thing that matters first and last. It was in their relationship to this all-important matter that the various forms of arrhythmia had to be considered ; it was by their effect on the efficiency of the heart that their importance had to be judged. It was not long before the value of auscultatory signs was weighed. Murmurs had for decades been studied and described. Their real significance was assessed by Mackenzie, who correlated their presence with the effect that the lesions causing them had on the heart's capacity for work. The reserve power of the myocardium was the real thing that mattered. The study of the understanding of the response of the heart to effort engaged him for a long time. In this he turned back once more to the minute and intimate investigation of the patient's symptoms : the point from which he had started years before. Inevitably this involved an enquiry into the nature of that most important of all cardiac symptoms, angina pectoris. Our later knowledge has carried us here rather further than he went. But his conclusions were not far off the mark. It was exhaustion of the heart muscle that mattered.

Mackenzie came to London in 1906, at the age of fifty-four. His great book, "Diseases of the Heart," was published about this time. There is no space to deal with the more personal details of his life—they have been well recorded by those who knew him. Rather has an attempt been made to show how observation, reasoning and the testing of ideas, the following of the true clues with unerring instinct, led to the knowledge that forms the basis of nearly all the important part of our modern conceptions concerning the diseases of the heart. But apart from these steps already traced, Mackenzie was indefatigable in his enquiries into the mechanism of the production of symptoms.

The question of referred pain engaged him, and he investigated the surface distribution of pain from the internal viscera.

His rapid accession to the position of first authority on cardiac disease is known to all. From the London Hospital, the staff of which he was invited to join, he preached the supreme importance of the efficiency of the heart muscle as the criterion by which the importance of all abnormalities must be judged.

But in spite of this his mind was ever searching at the problem which had first engaged him years before. The nature and origin of the early symptoms of disease was a riddle, the solution of which in so many cases had hardly been approached. At the age of sixty-five he left London to set out upon the quest. He chose St. Andrews as the suitable place—not too large and not too small, where the population was stationary—in which to start his investigation of the earliest manifestations of disease. The general practitioners of the area were to work in conjunction with him. The James Mackenzie Institute of Clinical Research was started. But the time was growing short. The symptoms of angina pectoris became manifest. In 1924 the disease, the nature of which he had done so much to make clear, claimed him as a victim.

This short sketch can only be inadequate, but it conveys some small idea of the remarkable achievement of a great man. When one considers how much light he threw into what was one of the darkest corners of medicine, working single-handed against so many difficulties, one is left filled with humble admiration for his many great qualities, all the greater for the fact that they were founded upon a basis of fine humanity.

T. E.

E. H. STARLING
1866–1927

Bronze Bust executed in Italy in 1918.

To face p. 221

XXIV ERNEST HENRY STARLING
(1866–1927)
PHYSIOLOGIST

FEW Englishmen have contributed more to the scientific background of modern medicine than Starling. A man of unusually strong character and great personal charm, wide vision and colossal energy, his mark was made very largely by reason of the power he possessed of influencing and inspiring all those whose good fortune it was to come into contact with him.

Ernest Henry Starling was born in London on April 17th, 1866, and was the eldest son of H. H. Starling, a practising barrister and Clerk to the Crown in Bombay, and author of a work on Indian legal procedure. The family of seven was educated in England, the children being brought up by their mother, a woman of outstanding mental character and personal charm, from whom many of Starling's personal traits were said to have been inherited. He was educated at King's College School, matriculating with honours at the London University at the age of sixteen and a half, and in 1883 entered Guy's Hospital. Always an eager personality, he had a brilliant career as a student.

Highly imaginative, and by no means unromantic, the great generalisations of biology appealed strongly to him in his student days, for at about that time the broad principles of Darwinism, established after bitter struggle, were being received in a more critical manner ; and the work of Weissmann, De Vries, and others, which was to bring about considerable modification in our views of the origin of species, were already in the air. Generalisations on the grand scale, as opposed to niggling detail, always had a great fascination for him. It was the noble and sweeping gesture of nineteenth-century biology, dominated by the controversy around the theory of evolution, which impressed him much more than the minutiæ of contemporary biological teaching, and which, indeed, lastingly coloured his whole biological outlook.

Although it was his original intention to become a physician, his natural craving for exact knowledge on the one hand and his early and growing belief in the power with which physiological knowledge might be applied to the conquest of suffering on the other, attracted him to physiology while he was still a medical student. Perusal of one of his notebooks, dated 1883, shows that at the age of seventeen he had already approached physiology with an intensity very different from that of the average medical student. In its pages one recognises phrases and points of view characteristic of him in later life, and sufficient in themselves to place him well above the heads of most of his contemporaries.

When a student, Starling was taught organic chemistry by Dr. Debus, and was much influenced by that lucid expositor. Liebig and Wöhler had then only recently passed away, and it was already being recognised that organic chemistry was likely to play an important part in future developments of medical and biological science —how great a part was perhaps then hardly realised. Although, so far as the writer is aware, he never acquired any depth in the actual technique of chemistry, he was always alive to its physiological applications, and it is not surprising that while a student he gained, among other distinctions, an exhibition and gold medal in chemistry as well as in physiology. Some time about 1886 he interrupted his studies to spend a few months in W. Kühne's laboratory at Heidelberg. Kühne's important monograph on albumoses and peptones appeared at about that time, and Starling returned, as his old friend Sir Charles Martin remarks, "with his hair *en brosse* and much teutonised." The ideas of the fundamental importance of physiology and of the significance to it of chemistry had now become convictions, which only grew in intensity as they were vindicated by his subsequent experience. The acquaintance with the German language which he made on that visit, and which he afterwards took every advantage to enlarge, stood him in good stead in after years, for he spoke German well and with evident delight.

Graduating in Medicine in the University of London in 1888, he became a demonstrator in Physiology at Guy's Hospital, and was associated there with L. C. Wooldridge, whom he greatly admired, and by whom he was much influenced. Their collaboration was abruptly terminated by Wooldridge's tragic death a year later, and Starling was then appointed a part-time lecturer in Physiology, jointly with Golding Bird and Washbourne. In 1890, shortly after receiving this appointment, he gained the M.D. London. The salary attached to the joint lectureship at Guy's, and intended as a part-time salary for one person, being now divided, was insufficient for subsistence, and there is little doubt that but for the timely help which he received by the tenure, in 1891–2, of a British Medical Association scholarship, and later from a Grocers' scholarship and from examinerships, he would probably have been compelled to turn to other channels in search of a livelihood and to enable him to marry.

His marriage to Florence, widow of Wooldridge and daughter of a distinguished physician, Sir Edward Sieveking, took place in 1891. (Incidentally, it was Sieveking who, in 1877, in a letter to his friend, Sharpey, first drew attention to the now famous passage in Harvey's 1616 lecture notes, then recently discovered by the British Museum officials, and in which Harvey compares the action of the valves of the heart to the "clack of a water-bellows.") There had been a daughter by her first marriage, and there were to be three daughters and a son to Starling. It would be unfair to speak of Starling's career without further reference to Mrs. Starling. A woman of keen intelligence, speaking German fluently and abounding with nervous energy, with a heart overflowing with kindness and filled with devotion to him and her children, she was of the greatest help to him, particularly in the preparation of his books and papers during their earlier years of struggle. She translated from the German the fourth edition of Bunge's "Physiological Chemistry" (1902). Numerous friends still recall her kind and happy hospitality for many years at their home at 40 West End Lane, and also afterwards, when they grew older and needed less space, at 23 Taviton Street.

In 1892 Starling paid a second visit to Germany, this time to work at Breslau with Rudolf Heidenhain. Heidenhain, a pupil and son-in-law of Volkmann and a former associate of Du Bois Reymond, was then a distinguished man, fifty-eight years of age; to him Starling had no doubt gone, as he had gone to Kühne, on the earlier advice of Wooldridge; through Heidenhain's connections, Starling made contact with a great and fertile period of physiological research in Germany. Moreover, working as assistants in Heidenhain's laboratory at that time were Hürthle, Röhmann and Kramer, from all of whom he gained a great deal. After this visit he resumed work in the medical school at Guy's Hospital.

The accommodation at Guy's Hospital in the early

nineties being inadequate, Starling made arrangements to carry out part of his research work in Schäfer's laboratory at University College, which, though meagrely furnished according to present-day standards, was, nevertheless, much superior. The hospitality which he received at University College was fortunate for him, and for physiology, in more ways than one, for it was here that he made the close acquaintance of W. M. Bayliss, who had returned there from Oxford about 1890, and so began that remarkable partnership which lasted for so many years. Schäfer's colleagues were an enthusiastic group. Bayliss was then working on the depressor nerve ; in the laboratory were also Haliburton, Sydney Ringer, Rose Bradford, Leonard Hill, Marcet, and, later, Benjamin Moore and Swale Vincent.

Among Starling's achievements must be numbered the material improvements which he brought about in the schools with which he was connected. Never content to give way to obstacles of any sort, he agitated for the improvement of the laboratories at Guy's, and by 1895 a scheme for the reconstruction of the physiological laboratory had been approved. The resulting department, completed in 1897, and incorporating ideas culled from his continental visits, was then the best in London. He enjoyed its facilities for only a short time, however, for on Schäfer's move to the chair of Physiology at Edinburgh in 1899, Starling was appointed to succeed him in the Jodrell Chair of Physiology at University College, London.

Here he was able permanently to join his friend Bayliss, who six years previously had married his sister, Gertrude Starling. The laboratory at University College was then situated in the North Wing of the College, now occupied by the Botanical Department. Shortly after his arrival as head of the department at University College, the whole

16

country was roused by the action for libel and slander which was taken and won by Bayliss against the Hon. Stephen Coleridge, secretary of an anti-vivisection society. The sum of £2,000 awarded at the verdict given on November 18th, 1903, and which was greeted in the court with "loud and prolonged applause," was generously given to the department by Bayliss, and the invested sum still yields a revenue. The College at that time was in financial difficulties, and once more Starling found himself in premises which seemed to him unworthy, and to the improvement of which he set his mind and energy. By this time his views had become much more ambitious, and he envisaged the creation of a large institute of medical sciences in which anatomy, histology, embryology, physiology, biochemistry and pharmacology should be housed. Each department was to be in connection with the remainder and with the School of Advanced Medical Studies which dealt with clinical work. The first phase in the realisation of this dream was accomplished, very largely through his efforts and by means of money raised by him in 1909, when the nucleus of the present department was opened. An adjoining pharmacology department was added four years later, and in 1923, by the generosity of the Rockefeller Foundation, there was added the department of anatomy, histology and embryology, together with an extension of the physiology department, which more than doubled its original research accommodation. It would seem that he now realised that having materialised his vision of a large department, its size would mean that, at his age of fifty-seven, and with his reserves of strength lowered by the severe operation which he had undergone in June, 1920, too much of his energy would be absorbed in administering it. The increase in the accommodation provided by the new extension can be best illustrated by the change in the numbers of staff and attached research workers which occurred during the fourteen years which intervened between the erection of the original "Institute of physiology," in 1909, and the extended department created in 1923. In 1910 there were about twelve research workers and teachers in the department of physiology and biochemistry; its capacity in 1923 was at least forty, and it has at times held upwards of fifty workers. With a reasonable expectation of many active years still to come, he accordingly, and very wisely, accepted in 1922 the appointment to a Foulerton Research Professorship of the Royal Society, to be taken up in 1923. Not wishing to sever himself from University College, however, he arranged for a suitable suite of rooms to be provided in the extension which was being built, and in this suite he remained, and led a devoted band of research workers until shortly before his death. It was a sad blow to him that his colleague, Bayliss, died a year after he had taken up this Foulerton Chair.

By no means the least important of Starling's contributions to the physiological literature of his day were various text-books and addresses. Already, by 1892, he had produced the "Elements of Human Physiology," the well-known "green book," which ran through eight editions before it was allowed to lapse in 1907. In 1904, a primer, remarkable for its clarity and directness, appeared. The great work, "Principles of Human Physiology," which it had long been his ambition to produce in replacement of the "Elements," first appeared in 1912, and four editions and a Spanish translation had appeared by 1925. Other important books were the two volumes of Mercers' Company lectures on "Recent Advances in the Physiology of Digestion" (1906), and "Fluids of the Body" (1909); the Oliver-Sharpey Lectures on "The Feeding of Nations"

(1919), and "The Action of Alcohol on Man" (with other contributors)—1923.

Starling was well equipped by his training and by the personalities with which he came into contact to undertake a wide range of research problems. Kühne had carried out pioneer work on digestion, as is shown by the fact that he is credited with the introduction of such everyday words as "enzyme" and "trypsin." Heidenhain had extensively studied gastric and other secretions, and had invented a gastric pouch which his pupil Pavlov was later to improve upon; while his work on lymph formation, urinary secretion and absorption had given the mechanistic Ludwig school food for much thought; he had also worked on the innervation of the heart. Starling's most distinguished work was in similar directions on lymph formation, on various problems in digestion, on the circulatory system and on urinary secretion. His collaboration with Bayliss was most fruitful, for the two complemented one another: whereas Starling was eager and imaginative, but not naturally dexterous, and at times impatient, Bayliss, equally imaginative, was patient, philosophical, of immense learning, and delighted in mechanisms and in tasks involving manual skill. Although any natural gifts Starling may have had as a manipulator went largely uncultivated, since he was always willing to leave the details of construction of apparatus and preparation to his collaborators—for he seldom worked alone—he, nevertheless, acquired by sheer practice and determination, operative skill and dexterity of a high order. In his later years there were few physiological operations which he could not perform with the complete confidence and consummate skill of an artist.

His first few papers, written jointly with Bayliss, appeared in 1891–2, and dealt with the electromotive phenomena and innervation of the heart and with the accurate recording of endocardiac pressure curves. They showed that vagus stimulation definitely depresses the conduction of the excitatory process from auricle to ventricle, and were the first to use an optically-recorded system of high frequency and small mass for studying the endocardiac pressure changes.

During his stay at Breslau, Starling had, at Heidenhain's suggestion, undertaken a further study of the action of such lymphagogues as peptone. Heidenhain supposed that the increased lymph flow which followed the injection of peptone could only be explained by postulating an active secretion of lymph by the vessel walls. Although the experiments on which this view was based were all confirmed by Starling, either at Breslau or after his return to London, he became more and more dissatisfied with Heidenhain's explanation, and continued to work on the subject for five years. The outcome was that he ultimately realised that there must be some factor normally at work which opposed the blood pressure in the capillaries, but which could be reduced or abolished under certain conditions. This factor he found to be the osmotic pressure of the plasma proteins, which he measured and showed to be of the same order as the capillary pressure. It would be difficult to overrate the importance, both theoretical and practical, of this discovery, which at a stroke gave the key to many hitherto unexplained phenomena in physiology, and also shed a powerful light on the whole pathology of œdema and effusion production.

This investigation, exacting though it was, did not occupy his whole time, for there was heavy teaching work to be done at Guy's and problems of other sorts were also in hand. Among them were those connected with the innervation and movements of the alimentary canal. These experiments, begun at Guy's Hospital jointly with Bayliss, were continued by them at University College on Starling's transference thither. Their results provided a definite advance, and it seemed at the time that they had hit upon the only possible means of approach to the study of the movements of the alimentary canal. It happened, however, that in the same year as their work on this subject was begun (1898), another physiologist, W. B. Cannon, of Harvard, had introduced the use of the then recently-discovered X-rays, combined with an opaque meal, for following the movements of the alimentary canal. The initiation of this valuable method, which was soon to be adapted for use in man, together with the results simultaneously obtained on dogs by Bayliss and Starling, speedily brought the technique and knowledge of the subject almost to the point which it occupies to-day.

Bayliss and Starling now turned their attention to an apparently anomalous instance of pancreatic secretion in response to the introduction of acid into the intestine, an investigation which led in 1902 to the discovery of secretin. It is probably for this work that they are both most widely known, and for which they will be longest remembered, for by introducing the conception of the hormones it marked a new phase of physiological thought which has since developed innumerable ramifications.

After some further joint work on pancreatic juice and its activation by enterokinase, Bayliss and Starling took different paths, for the work on the pancreas had led Bayliss to an intensive study, on physico-chemical lines, of enzyme action and adsorption, while Starling was busy planning the new Institute of Physiology and with the many details of building and equipment which this entailed. It is doubtless unfortunate that they never actually collaborated in publication again. As soon as the new department was finished, Starling began work on experimental problems connected with asphyxia, and in this he was soon joined by a group of enthusiastic visitors for whom the laboratory now offered ample space.

The work was shortly interrupted by a serious breakdown in health in 1910. Much overworked by the occupation of the new laboratories, he was finally exhausted by attending an International Congress of Physiology at Vienna in the late summer of 1910; with the intention of recuperating, he had then gone on to the Dolomites to indulge in his favourite pastime of climbing. The unusual exertion caused an acute cardiac dilatation from which he nearly succumbed, and which made him an invalid for several months. Early in 1911, however, he recovered sufficiently to take a voyage to Japan, from which he returned filled with his wonted vigour.

What was probably his most productive period now followed. With increased staff, ample accommodation, new equipment and a rapidly-growing band of diligent helpers, his most earnest desire had been fulfilled. Investigators from all parts of the world soon flocked to him and work went on apace. One of the first achievements was the introduction in 1912 of the heart-lung preparation by Knowlton and Starling. Previous attempts had been made to secure a similar working isolated mammalian heart preparation—the most notable perhaps being that of Newell Martin in 1883—but for various reasons these had met with only limited success. The success and the simplicity of the Starling preparation enabled a number of valuable researches to be made on the heart—particularly on the coronary circulation, on the oxygen usage of the heart, normal and diabetic, and on the response of the heart to increased work. The importance of the latest named research, carried out largely in conjunction with

S. W. Patterson, afterwards Starling's son-in-law, was great. It soon came to be realised that a physiological dilatation of the heart was a normal occurrence in exercise.

This happy International party: Russians, Germans, Japanese and members of British Dominions, was scattered by the sweeping blow of war in 1914. Starling's energies were now directed with his usual enthusiasm into channels of war service. Carried away by the war fever, he heroically attempted to acquire a good knowledge of French, which he naturally abhorred, and to forget his German, in which he had found such pleasure. Nor was he the only one who did such things, afterwards acknowledged to be strange. In the early days he was with difficulty restrained from joining a fighting branch of the services; ultimately he was prevailed upon to join the R.A.M.C., in which, with the rank of Captain, he was drafted as a medical officer to the Herbert Hospital.

The initiation of gas warfare in 1915, however, gave opportunities for a better form of service, and early in 1916 he was given the rank of Major, and made director of anti-gas research work, then centred at Millbank. Here he saw the invention of the box respirator, largely the work of the late E. F. Harrison; but for his energy the adoption of this form of protection would doubtless have been long delayed. Becoming impatient of official methods, and being therefore somewhat of an embarrassment to the authorities, on June 30th, 1916, he was promoted to the rank of Lieutenant-Colonel and sent out to Salonika as Army chemical adviser with nothing to do. Feeling that he had been side-tracked, he resigned his Commission in 1917, and returned as a civilian, and so with more power to be of use.

The shortage of food in England had by that time become serious, and the Government was compelled to seek expert advice; the appointment of Starling as Chairman of the Royal Society's Food Committee enabled him once more to render valuable service, which was further enhanced when he was appointed scientific adviser to the Ministry of Food and British Scientific Delegate on the Inter-Allied Food Commission.

Once more, early in 1918, he was requisitioned by the War Office, this time as a civilian emissary, to negotiate with the Italian authorities the supply of British box respirators to the Italian forces. The time was spent at Padua, Rome, and at the Italian Commando Supremo, and culminated in the supply of one and a quarter million respirators to the Italian Forces. The officer who accompanied him on this mission, and who helped to smuggle him across the frontier at Modane when he lost his passport on the way back, was much intrigued by a heavy box which he brought back from Rome. Only after Starling's death was it revealed that this contained a bronze bust of himself made in Rome at Professor Fano's suggestion.

The War ended shortly after the return from this mission and, returning to University College, he took up further work on the circulation. With Anrep and other colleagues he extended our knowledge of the coronary circulation and of the central control of the circulation. In 1920 he went on an academic mission to India, and there contracted a slight attack of malaria; worse was to follow, however, for on his return journey symptoms of intestinal obstruction appeared, and these necessitated an operation for carcinoma immediately on his return to England in June, 1920. Two attacks of pulmonary embolism marked the recovery from this, and he was then more or less incapacitated and crippled by protracted attacks of intermittent claudication affecting a leg. Ultimately he made a good recovery, continued his work, supervised the building of the new extensions, and took over the Foulerton Research Chair. His work was now eased by the removal of administrative duties, so that henceforward research work was intensive. It was chiefly directed to work on urinary secretion, employing the heart-lung-kidney preparation, and to further researches on the energy expenditure of the heart, in both of which researches the heart-lung preparation was employed.

By 1923 his health seemed re-established, and his bright exuberance restored. This state continued until early in 1927; but shortly after a period of exceptionally heavy work, culminating in an Annual General Meeting of the Physiological Society, he suddenly collapsed, in March, 1927. After some measure of improvement he decided to try another sea voyage, and in April started from Bristol for Jamaica on board the "Ariguani." Quite suddenly, as the ship neared Kingston, he died on April 30th, and was buried at St. Andrew's Parish Church, Halfway Tree, a few miles out of Kingston, on the following day.

Starling received many honours and distinctions. Honorary degrees were conferred on him by the Universities of Dublin, Sheffield and Cambridge, and by the two German Universities of Breslau and Heidelberg, in which he studied. He became a Fellow of the Royal Society in 1899, served three times on its Council, and was awarded the Baly Medal in 1901 and the Royal Medal in 1913. He was elected a Fellow of the Royal College of Physicians in 1897. The C.M.G. was a war award for his services at Salonika, but he received no other recognition from the State for his many other services.

Starling was greatly beloved by his colleagues and by his very many pupils. The alert and unflinching gaze of blue eyes beneath heavy eyebrows, the smile that so often lit up with extraordinary charm and attraction a face otherwise set in a serious mould by long and arduous study, will endure to the end in the memories of all who knew him. He had unusual gifts of eloquence and clear vision both in his oral and written teaching ; he gave freely and of his best to all those who came to him for help in the difficulties of their work for physiology ; he gave too with patience, with modesty and with a rare courtesy.

C. L. E.

INDEX